Crimes Against Humanity
Humanity
A Beginner's Guide

ONEWORLD BEGINNER'S GUIDES combine an original, inventive, and engaging approach with expert analysis on subjects ranging from art and history to religion and politics, and everything in between. Innovative and affordable, books in the series are perfect for anyone curious about the way the world works and the big ideas of our time.

anarchism
ruth kinna

anti-capitalism
simon tormey

artificial intelligence
blay whitby

the bahá'í faith
moojan momen

the beat generation
christopher gair

biodiversity
john spicer

bioterror & biowarfare
malcolm dando

the brain
a. al-chalabi, m. r. turner
& r. s. delamont

christianity
keith ward

cloning
aaron d. levine

criminal psychology
ray bull *et al.*

crimes against humanity
adam jones

daoism
james miller

democracy
david beetham

energy
vaclav smil

evolution
burton s. guttman

evolutionary psychology
r. dunbar, l.barrett &
j. lycett

existentialism
thomas e. wartenberg

fair trade
jacqueline decarlo

genetics
a. griffiths, b.guttman,
d. suzuki & t. cullis

global terrorism
leonard weinberg

hinduism
klaus k. klostermaier

life in the universe
lewis dartnell

mafia & organized crime
james o. finckenauer

marx
andrew collier

medieval philosophy
sharon m. kaye

NATO
jennifer medcalf

oil
vaclav smil

the palestine–israeli conflict
dan cohn-sherbok &
dawoud el-alami

paul
morna d. hooker

philosophy of mind
edward feser

postmodernism
kevin hart

psychology
g. neil martin

quantum physics
alastair i. m. rae

racism
alana lentin

religion
martin forward

the small arms trade
m. schroeder, r. stohl
& d. smith

sufism
william c. chittick

SELECTED FORTHCOMING TITLES:

astronomy
british politics
censorship
civil liberties
classics
climate change
ethics

feminism
globalization
history of science
humanism
journalism
literary theory
middle east

modern slavery
philosophy of religion
racism
renaissance art
romanticism
shakespeare
socialism

Crimes Against Humanity
A Beginner's Guide

Adam Jones

ONEWORLD

OXFORD

A Oneworld Book

Published by Oneworld Publications 2008

Copyright © Adam Jones 2008

ISBN 978–1–85168–601–8

Typeset by Jayvee, Trivandrum, India
Cover design by Simon McFadden
Printed and bound in Great Britain by
TJ International, Padstow, Cornwall

Oneworld Publications
185 Banbury Road
Oxford OX2 7AR
England
www.oneworld-publications.com

Mixed Sources
Product group from well-managed
forests and other controlled sources
www.fsc.org Cert no. SGS-COC-2482
© 1996 Forest Stewardship Council
FSC

To Mentors
Rex Brynen • Kal Holsti • Ben Kiernan

About ...

the cover image

Near the village of San Francisco Javier in the Quiché highlands, Guatemala, 2000. Two sisters watch the exhumation of their mother and four small siblings. The sisters were present in August of 1982 when soldiers shot their relatives, but they managed to escape. Carrying what they could, they had fled with others from their community after hearing a massacre taking place in a neighboring village. Two hours later, they were surprised by a Guatemalan army patrol that opened fire on the group, killing thirty-six people. Together with their brother, the sisters spent fourteen years in hiding in the mountains, living with the Communities of Population in Resistance (CPR) of the Sierra, before resettling in a new community and later petitioning for the exhumation.

the photographer

Jonathan Moller has spent most of the last fifteen years working as a human rights advocate and freelance photographer in Guatemala, principally with indigenous Maya populations uprooted by that country's long and brutal internal conflict. In 2000 and 2001, he worked for a Guatemalan forensic anthropology team that documented the exhumations of clandestine cemeteries, searching for the remains of a few of the more than 250,000 civilians killed or 'disappeared' during the Guatemalan army's genocidal campaign of the early 1980s. His photographs from Guatemala have been widely exhibited and published, used by many NGOs and educational institutions, and collected in a number of museums. His first book, *Our Culture Is Our Resistance: Repression, Refuge and Healing in Guatemala*, was published in English by powerHouse Books and in Spanish by Turner Libros.

Contents

Preface viii

Acknowledgments xv

Illustrations xvi

1 **Genesis** 1

2 **Genocide and extermination** 19

3 **Forced population transfer and 'ethnic cleansing'** 40

4 **Slavery and human trafficking** 57

5 **Arbitrary imprisonment** 74

6 **Torture** 90

7 **Rape and sexual crimes** 105

8 **Forced disappearance** 121

9 **Apartheid** 132

Conclusion 151

Further reading 158

Index 164

Preface

This book is the first primer on crimes against humanity aimed at a general audience. Previous efforts have been overwhelmingly legal-philosophical in tone and content. It would hardly make sense to jettison a legal framing for what are, after all, defined as *crimes* against humanity. I devote much of chapter 1 to the subject, and hope that the portrait of legal definitions, mechanisms, and institutions in this short volume is accurate and illuminating. However, I cast a wider net, examining crimes against humanity from a social-scientific perspective, principally a political science and international relations one. In particular, I explore crimes against humanity as a set of *prohibition regimes*: attempts to entrench norms in international politics and society that proscribe a given practice.

A prohibition regime is simply an international or global 'Thou shalt not'. In this book, the injunctions are along the lines of: Thou shalt not commit torture. Thou shalt not persecute, ethnically cleanse, racially oppress, rape, or forcibly impregnate. These acts are relevant in the present context to the extent that they have prompted a coherent drive to brand them as crimes against humanity, and to outlaw and suppress them.

Like other moral injunctions, prohibition regimes focusing on crimes against humanity vary widely in their effectiveness. Some – against slavery, for example – have established themselves so solidly that a resurgence of the phenomenon as a legal international practice is scarcely conceivable, though illicit pockets exist at the national level, and associated practices (human trafficking, indentured labor, forced labor) are still widespread. It is likewise unthinkable that apartheid, as a formal structure of rule, could be re-established in South Africa.

In other cases – genocide, say, or forced disappearance, or sexual violence against women – the prohibition regime is at best loosely institutionalized, and relatively weak in capacity. Hands may be wrung and rhetorical energy expended, but policing and practical interventions are limited, and the phenomenon in question remains endemic.

Nonetheless, broadly viewed, the notion that systematic crimes against civilians are atrocities against all 'humanity', which is in turn obliged to monitor, suppress, and punish them, has grown incrementally but inexorably, especially in recent decades. That it has done so is the result of coalitions of individuals, mass publics, materially or symbolically powerful states, and various other governmental and nongovernmental agents. The story of how citizens band together into 'principled issue networks' to establish or defend a norm is sometimes a story of paternalism or Western neocolonialism. More often, though, it is one of the most inspiring narratives in the human record. Addressing crimes against humanity necessarily forces us into vicarious contact with some of history's worst atrocities. But it also introduces us to shining inspirations, such as:

- The religious activists and former slaves who organized in the late eighteenth and early nineteenth centuries to abolish slavery as a legal and global trade;
- Raphael Lemkin, the Polish refugee who developed the concept of 'genocide' in the early 1940s, and within only a few years persuaded the United Nations to adopt an international convention outlawing the practice;
- Amnesty International, which defends political prisoners against torture and unlawful confinement by relentlessly publicizing the crimes of their persecutors, becoming one of the world's most influential nongovernmental organizations (NGOs);

- The Mothers of the Disappeared, whose weekly demonstrations in the central square of Buenos Aires for years represented the only visible and public opposition to the Argentine military dictatorship;
- Nelson Mandela and the African National Congress, who led a decades-long struggle to overthrow South African apartheid.

These individuals and organizations offer vivid evidence that, in philosopher John Stuart Mill's dictum, 'one person with a belief is a social power equal to ninety-nine who have only interests'. Or, as the anthropologist Margaret Mead put it: 'Never doubt that a small group of thoughtful, committed citizens can change the world. Indeed, it is the only thing that ever has.'

The upheavals that these individuals and institutions sparked have their origins in 'catalyzing ideas' that convey a new sense of what is possible. 'Crimes against humanity', when you consider it closely, is one of the more remarkable notions yet conceived. How does a violent and oppressive action or practice come to be viewed as violating not only the rights and integrity of the direct victim, but indirectly those of all humanity? What is the emergent (cosmopolitan) identity that grants a universal entity – humanity – a capacity to be injured by such acts, and a right to prevent and punish them?

In exploring the catalyzing ideas that helped galvanize movements against torture, apartheid, or women's oppression, I want to attend to *how* those progressive messages have been communicated and disseminated. If one believer can outweigh ninety-nine of the merely interested, then a believer with a megaphone – a way of amplifying his or her public presence – can be even more influential. Campaigns to prohibit abuse and atrocity nearly always have sophisticated outreach and 'marketing' strategies. International organizations, notably the United Nations system, provide vital resources for generating and sharing information, as well as meeting, interacting, and cross-pollinating. And we will pay special heed to the 'ideational' component of these movements: the media workers, 'public intellectuals', writers, and artists who have broadened the scope of human possibility through their sympathetic engagement with others, real and fictitious. In her incisive recent study, *Inventing Human Rights*, historian Lynn Hunt shows how the eighteenth-century novel allowed readers to transcend traditional barriers of gender and social 'station', arriving at a newly universalistic 'sense of equality and empathy' (see Box below).

The examples could be multiplied. In the 1850s, Harriet Beecher Stowe electrified the English-speaking world with her

---

'NOVELS AND EMPATHY': LYNN HUNT

Novels like *Julie* [by Jean-Jacques Rousseau] drew their readers into identifying with ordinary characters, who were by definition unknown to the reader personally. Readers empathized with the characters, especially the heroine or hero, thanks to the workings of the narrative form itself. Through the fictional exchange of letters, in other words, epistolary novels taught their readers nothing less than a new psychology and in the process laid the foundations for a new social and political order . . . Novels made the point that all people are fundamentally similar because of their inner feelings, and many novels showcased in particular the desire for autonomy. In this way, reading novels created a sense of equality and empathy through passionate involvement in the narrative. Can it be coincidental that the three greatest novels of psychological identification of the eighteenth century – Richardson's *Pamela* (1740) and *Clarissa* (1747–48), and Rousseau's *Julie* (1761) – were all published in the period that immediately preceded the appearance of the concept of 'the rights of man'?

Lynn Hunt, *Inventing Human Rights: A History* (New York: W.W. Norton & Co., 2007), pp. 38–9.

novel *Uncle Tom's Cabin*, which laid bare the crimes of slavery. In less than two years, 1.5 million copies were in print. E. D. Morel's *Red Rubber* ripped the lid off atrocities in the Belgian Congo in the late nineteenth century and into the twentieth, helping to fuel one of the earliest and most successful international human-rights movements. Nowadays, songs, movies, and media reports are perhaps more significant in 'spreading the word' and helping to forge popular movements. Think of Bob Marley, with his hymns of love and liberation, incarnating the liberation struggle of colonized and once-colonized peoples everywhere. Or the brave reporters who took to the field in Bosnia-Herzegovina during the early 1990s, and brought back indelible images of concentration camps, mass destruction, and haunted refugees that finally prompted a measure of Western intervention (see chapter 3). This book tries to do some justice to these creative works, and reproduces a few eloquent images along the way.

Outline of the book

This book had its beginnings as a proposal from the publisher to write a beginner's guide to genocide. Several short overviews already existed, however, while I had written what sought to be a 'comprehensive introduction' to the subject. I suggested instead a focus on crimes against humanity. One intriguing question, however, is whether genocide itself is to be considered a crime against humanity. I will argue that it should be, and I include it under that rubric here. The treatment of genocide in chapter 2 is twinned with an officially recognized crime against humanity, extermination, which preceded it in international law. (Extermination was used at Nuremberg in 1945–7 to cover many of the crimes that would subsequently be enumerated in the Genocide Convention.)

The Rome Statute of the International Criminal Court (ICC) occupies a special position in the book. As the best reflection of the prevailing international consensus on crimes against humanity (and war crimes, and genocide), it is a touchstone that will only grow in importance in coming years. The crimes against humanity enumerated in the Statute compose the general structure of this book, and 'Elements of Crimes', a supplementary document to the Statute, is also most helpful in illustrating core international-legal understandings. But, to repeat, I use legal materials and framings instrumentally throughout this book, to assist in illuminating more diverse arguments and explorations. There is already a good, albeit small, legal literature on crimes against humanity. It is utilized throughout this text, and referenced in the Further Reading for chapter 1; interested readers should have no trouble tracking down the core works.

In each chapter, I try to present a particular crime as a historical-social phenomenon, an evolving legal concept, and an active site of popular mobilization. I have also sprinkled the volume with box-texts, in which core documents are cited, and useful authorities – whether participants, witnesses, or analysts – are granted a say.

About crimesagainsthumanity.ca

The website crimesagainsthumanity.ca accompanies this book. It features a range of additional materials for students, teachers, and general readers. These include complete references for the volume; an appendix providing excerpts from primary documents (e.g., human rights instruments) cited in the book, with links to their full text; questions for classroom discussion; a filmography of genocide and crimes against humanity; a compendium of current reportage; and other resources.

References

For reasons of digestibility, references are not included in this volume, beyond the suggestions for further reading compiled at the end. Complete references are available in the notes section of crimesagainsthumanity.ca, or by email from the author at adamj_jones@hotmail.com

Acknowledgments

In the spirit of a primer, I will keep this brief. I am very grateful to Marsha Filion at Oneworld Publications, who first invited me to write a 'Beginner's Guide' on genocide, and with her fellow editors was receptive when I suggested instead an accessible, non-technical volume on crimes against humanity. I hope we shall work together again.

This book owes a great deal to the two years, 2005–7, that I spent on a postdoctoral fellowship in the Genocide Studies Program at Yale University. Sharpening my understanding of genocide served to deepen my interest in crimes against humanity – a parallel concept in many ways, yet intriguingly different in others. Heartfelt thanks to Ben Kiernan, director of the Genocide Studies Program, and to the staff of the MacMillan Center at Yale. Thanks also to Frederick J. Iseman, whose donation to the Yale Genocide Studies Program substantially funded the postdoctoral fellowship that brought me to Yale.

My parents, Jo and David Jones, and my Yale colleague and dear friend Benjamin Madley, went through the draft manuscript with a fine-toothed comb. Every page reflects their input, corrections, and suggested rephrasings. May I always have such meticulous advance readers to save me from myself. I accept full responsibility for any errors of fact and interpretation that remain.

The book was written at the outset of my employment as Associate Professor of Political Science at the University of British Columbia Okanagan. Thanks to my new colleagues, and to the family and friends who supply constant love and support.

Illustrations

Figure 1 Cree-Canadian singer Buffy Sainte-Marie symbolized the resurgence of Native pride and identity in North America in the 1960s and '70s. (Courtesy Buffy Sainte-Marie)   23

Figure 2 Bosnian Muslim women attending the annual memorial ceremony for victims of the July 1995 Srebrenica massacre, at the cemetery and memorial site built at the village of Potocari, Bosnia and Herzegovina. About 8,000 Muslim men and boys were massacred by Bosnian Serb paramilitary forces. (Adam Jones photo)   51

Figure 3 Detail of the famous diagram of Africans packed like sardines into the hold of the slave ship *Brookes*. The image was distributed around much of the world from the early 19th century as a vivid exemplar of slavery's horrors.   59

Figure 4 Russian map of the Gulag camp system, showing its extent across the length and breadth of the Soviet Union. The major network in the northeast includes the Kolyma gold fields, where many of the most murderous camps were located. (Copyright Memorial, Russia, with the assistance of the Feltrinelli foundation and staff of the Faculty of Geography and Cartography of Moscow State University, http://www.memo.ru)   78

Figure 5 A Gestapo torture chamber drawn by Karl Schwesig, who was imprisoned by the Nazis in the 1930s. (Courtesy Gallerie Remmert und Barth, Düsseldorf)   93

Figure 6 Map of apartheid-era South Africa, showing the Black 'homelands' (such as Transkei and Bophuthatswana) created on barren territories to provide an illusion of African political autonomy.   136

Figure 7 Global apartheid. (Courtesy Africa Action, www.africaaction.org)   147

1

Genesis

Spring 1915. World War I has degenerated into a grim war of attrition. Millions of soldiers are stuck fast in a trench system that snakes from the Belgian coast to the Swiss border.

In an attempt to break the deadlock, the British, French, and Anzac (Australia/New Zealand) forces launched an attack on the Dardanelles straits, seeking to force a way through to Constantinople and to neutralize the Ottoman Empire, a key German and Austrian ally. Partly in response to the crisis, the Ottoman authorities in Constantinople clamped down – not in the Dardanelles, but against the Christian minority populations of the empire: the Armenians, the Assyrians, the Anatolian and Pontian Greeks. What became known as 'the Armenian genocide' began with the arrest and eventual execution of hundreds of Armenian notables in the Ottoman capital and elsewhere. Brazen massacres of Armenians, Greeks, and Assyrians erupted across the realm, peaking between 1915 and 1917.

Seeking to assert its historic self-image as protector of Christian minorities in its sphere of influence, Russia called for a declaration by the countries of the Triple Entente alliance stating that the atrocities unleashed against the Armenians and others would be punished after an Entente victory. Great Britain and France were concerned that the Russian declaration, which referred to 'crimes . . . against Christianity and civilization', would only provoke further anti-Christian persecution, when the Allies could do nothing practical to assist the targeted populations. Accordingly, they pushed for a revision of the text. Sergei Sazonov, the Russian foreign minister, agreed to change the reference to crimes against *Christianity* to denounce instead

'HOLD PERSONALLY RESPONSIBLE': THE ALLIED DECLARATION OF MAY 1915

For about a month the Kurd and Turkish population of Armenia has been massacring Armenians with the connivance and often assistance of Ottoman authorities. Such massacres took place in middle April . . . at Erzerum, Dertchun, Eguine, Van, Bitlis, Mush, Sassun, Zeitun, and through Cilicia. Inhabitants of about one hundred villages near Van were all murdered. In that city [the] Armenian quarter is besieged by Kurds. At the same time in Constantinople [the] Ottoman Government ill-treats [the] inoffensive Armenian population. In view of these new crimes of Turkey against humanity and civilization, the Allied governments announce publicly to the Sublime Porte [Ottoman authorities] that they will hold personally responsible [for] these crimes all members of the Ottoman Government and those of their agents who are implicated in such massacres.

Quoted in Gary Jonathan Bass, *Stay the Hand of Vengeance: The Politics of War Tribunals* (Princeton, NJ: Princeton University Press, 2000), p. 117.

crimes '*against humanity and civilization*'. Thus, the drafters invented a phrase that 'was to become a powerful concept of international law – the "crime against humanity"'.

It would be easy to dismiss the Allies' declaration as merely wartime propaganda – or shameless hypocrisy. After all, as the leading colonial powers of the age, Britain and France had repeatedly slaughtered 'rebellious' civilian populations. Russia's treatment of its Caucasian Muslim population in the latter half of the nineteenth century was little less brutal and destructive than the Ottomans' campaign against their Christian subjects. It must also be acknowledged that the will to hold perpetrators accountable evaporated after a few trials were held in Constantinople in 1919–20. Nevertheless, the declaration built on centuries of evolving concepts of human rights – a growing sense of what would be called in the contemporary period 'the responsibility to protect'.

'Offend against all humankind'

> Discussions of crimes against humanity draw on both senses of the word 'humanity' – humanity as humanness and humanity as humankind. The central questions for any theory of crimes against humanity are how these deeds violate humanness and why they offend against all humankind.
>
> David Luban

Human beings have a highly developed capacity for *empathy*: the power to apprehend and commingle emotionally with another. This tends to be strongly focused at the epicenter of social organization, however – family, tribe, now extended to nation-state – and weaker with regard to those more remote or alien from the individual or subgroup. Our finely tuned sense of boundaries and territoriality makes us highly prone to intraspecies *alienation*, as evidenced by our ability to inflict campaigns of barbarism and extermination upon out-group populations.

Human beings have instituted norms and rules from the earliest period of recorded history to govern interactions among this peculiarly sociable, particularly volatile species. A broad conception of solidarity has governed intragroup (familial/tribal) organization. A vision of universal solidarity also came into being at a fairly early point. It usually took religious form: a concept of universal fraternity within a community of worship. In Greco-Roman and other traditions one may also discern the seed of a secular conception of individual rights – for example, citizenship and property rights. This mix of religious and civic values, in the Western tradition at least, provided the foundation for whatever more extensive concept of solidarity could be established when circumstances permitted.

The story of the modern era – from approximately the fifteenth century on – is in great part one of circumstances permitting. The growing *extensiveness* of human communication occurred in the context of what we know today as *globalization*. Western explorers charted the world, and Western imperial authorities followed in their train. The result was destruction on an unprecedented scale, beginning with the mass death of indigenous peoples across huge swaths of the Americas and Australasia, and the imposition on survivors of Western systems of philosophy, religion, and socioeconomic organization. However, the modern period also marks the onset and development of a genuinely *cosmopolitan* vision of international affairs: one that took the old Greco-Roman model of citizenship and extended it to a supranational or even global scale. (Immanuel Kant's *Towards Perpetual Peace*, written in 1795, is generally considered the foundational text.) In the last century or two, 'the notion that the individual is a citizen of the world and, indeed, that the world might become his or her *polis*', or primary political unit, has 'materialized into reality' with the growing number of people 'able to travel and find out about the world' combined with 'the economic expansion and the assertiveness of mass society' (Daniele Archibugi).

Lest this paint an overly rosy portrait of travelers and wayfarers spreading cosmopolitan norms worldwide, we must again stress that norms and international 'regimes' have usually been established as part and parcel of imperial expansion and hegemonic imposition. The nineteenth-century superpower, Great Britain, engineered the abolition of international slavery by devoting the resources to its suppression that Britain, and only Britain, could supply. United States sponsorship was essential in both the post-World War I and post-World War II periods to the formation of key international regimes, including the League of Nations and United Nations systems.

However, ideas and norms are not established in international society *merely* as projections of hegemonic power. First, they often result from actions taken in opposition to prevailing authority. Intraelite conflict – the rebellion of aristocrats against the King – produced the Magna Carta in the thirteenth century. The workers' and women's movements of the nineteenth and twentieth centuries established important benefits and protections for ordinary people in the Western world and beyond. And the twentieth century's greatest social movement – for decolonization and national liberation – entrenched the much-proclaimed, hitherto little-practiced norm of self-determination, along with prohibitions against colonial domination and forced racial segregation that are today among the most forceful of global prohibition regimes.

The movements that advanced these regimes were driven predominantly by nongovernmental actors, and in both the global South and the global North, such actors have sought to deepen and diversify bonds of human solidarity (and sometimes to undermine them through campaigns of hatred and political extremism). Nongovernmental organizations (NGOs) lobby, persuade, and shame states and other actors (e.g. multinational corporations) into compliance. They have also provided the expertise, especially scientific and legal, that underpins most of the international regimes currently extant.

Contemporary conceptions of human rights and 'crimes against humanity' center on the physical integrity of the individual. Violations of that integrity, particularly violent assaults, often evoke visceral empathy. Prohibition regimes against certain violations of rights are more likely to be sponsored and effectively regulated where they arouse widespread revulsion among publics and policymakers. When norm entrepreneurs can persuasively establish a connection between the practice and a serious physical violation, the requisite revulsion is most likely to be generated. This is the historical function of the diagram of the slave ship *Brookes* (chapter 4) or film footage of the Nazi concentration camps. In both cases, national and international opinion was shocked into institutional innovation in the field of human rights and (in the latter instance) 'crimes against humanity'.

In today's world, globalized communications are combined with a rich tapestry of international networks and institutions (both governmental and nongovernmental), and with an ever more cosmopolitan framing of human rights and physical integrity. Yet despite clear victories, many prohibition regimes to suppress particular crimes against humanity remain rudimentary at best. This is especially true when the cases are geographically and culturally distant from the Westernized center of the global order. The international community fiddles while genocide and ethnic cleansing sweep Darfur. One of the most vicious and systematic campaigns of mass rape ever recorded rages in Congo, provoking little more than occasional press reports and half-hearted peacekeeper interventions. Torture, established as an unusually potent prohibition regime by Western states in the nineteenth century, resurges in the 'war on terror', and the regime erodes.

Today, solidaristic/universalist/cosmopolitan perspectives contest the field with particularist/exclusivist conceptions. 'Crimes against humanity' is one of the most ringing expressions of the solidaristic view. There are grounds for believing that its progressive entrenching in international legal practice and public debate speaks to a relative increase in the human capacity for empathy and solidarity – though evidence for such general judgments is probably impossible to amass. Crimes against humanity are in essence crimes against one's fellows, viewed in a universal context. Human beings seem always to have been capable of feeling injury to one's fellow as an injury to oneself. We demonstrate a capacity to extend this empathy in communities of obligation that radiate outward from the self and core social unit, in circles of ever-greater inclusiveness. In their most contemporary and cosmopolitan conception, they encompass all of humanity – a humanity apprehended through unprecedentedly extensive webs of contact and channels of communication. The concept of crimes against humanity can therefore be expected to wax or wane in close connection with the broader appeal of a solidaristic conception and organization of human affairs.

Crimes against humanity in international law

By 1915, the notion of international human rights was well enough established that the Allies' declaration, however seriously intended, could land on receptive ears. The declaration at least serves as a marker of the evolution of 'human rights' from, and towards, a universal norm. In particular, it capped decades of mounting concern for the plight of religious and ethnic minorities in Ottoman-controlled south-eastern Europe.

The Martens Clause in the preamble of the 1899 Hague Conventions marked the first reference to 'the rule of the principles of the law of nations, as they result from the usages established among civilized peoples, *from the laws of humanity, and the dictates of the public conscience*' (emphasis added). Elsewhere, the Hague Conventions of 1899 and 1907 prohibited acts 'that "shock" the conscience of mankind. Or they "outrage" or "offend" the conscience, or the moral judgment, of mankind. Or they are "repugnant in the public conscience" or "intolerable from the point of view of the entire international community"; or they represent a challenge to the "imperatives", or the "law", or the "code", of "universal conscience"'.

These groundbreaking agreements paved the way for an impressive expansion of a universal rights discourse in the twentieth and twenty-first centuries. Before they did, however, human rights would be flouted on an unprecedented scale. In World War II, tens of millions of people were obliterated – as many as 40 million in the Soviet Union alone. By contrast with World War I, where mass atrocities against civilians were the exception rather than the rule, World War II established (or re-established) the principle of targeting the civilian population as a means of annihilating an implacable enemy. The Nazis genocided Jews, Roma (Gypsies), and Polish and Soviet Slavs. At home, and even before the war started, they targeted individuals according to political belief, physical or mental disability, and homosexuality, to cite just a handful of victim categories. The Japanese dropped plague bacilli on Chinese cities, and perpetrated numerous direct massacres. The Allies committed their own range of mass crimes against civilians, notably their indiscriminate bombing of urban areas. Germany and Japan had pioneered the practice; but it was discreetly left off the charge-sheet of the postwar tribunals, since the Allies had responded in kind with a ferocity – including atomic bombing – that dwarfed the original Axis assaults.

Among the victor's spoils claimed by the Allies at the onset of the postwar era was the right to try Nazi and Japanese leaders for war crimes and crimes against humanity. The result was the Nuremberg and Tokyo tribunals of 1945–7. Each proceeding, but especially Nuremberg, was among the most famous trials in history, a watershed in international jurisprudence, and a landmark toward accountability for perpetrators of mass atrocity. It was also at these trials that the concept of 'crimes against humanity' first found formal expression and codification, in language that has shaped interpretations ever since.

As the Box opposite outlines, ahead of crimes against humanity, Nuremberg's charter emphasized 'crimes against peace' – the wars of conquest that the Nazis waged – and the more widely accepted notion of 'war crimes'. This was typical of international legislation and covenant-framing to that point. By

THE NUREMBERG CHARTER: GENERAL PRINCIPLES (8 AUGUST 1945): ARTICLE 6

[. . .] The following acts, or any of them, are crimes coming within the jurisdiction of the Tribunal for which there shall be individual responsibility:

(a) *Crimes against peace:* namely, planning, preparation, initiation or waging of a war of aggression, or a war in violation of international treaties, agreements or assurances, or participation in a common plan or conspiracy for the accomplishment of any of the foregoing.

(b) *War crimes:* namely, violations of the laws or customs of war. Such violations shall include, but not be limited to, murder, ill-treatment or deportation to slave labor or for any other purpose, of civilian populations of or in occupied territory, murder or ill-treatment of prisoners of war or persons on the seas, killing of hostages, plunder of public or private property, wanton destruction of cities, towns or villages, or devastation not justified by military necessity.

(c) *Crimes against humanity:* namely, murder, extermination, enslavement, deportation, and other inhumane acts committed against any civilian population, before or during the war, or persecutions on political, racial or religious grounds in execution of or in connection with any crime within the jurisdiction of the Tribunal, whether or not in violation of the domestic law of the country where perpetrated.

Leaders, organizers, instigators and accomplices participating in the formulation or execution of a common plan or conspiracy to commit any of the foregoing crimes are responsible for all acts performed by any persons in execution of such plans.

including crimes against humanity, however, the Charter's framers sought to fill a void in international law: the failure adequately to address atrocious policies 'which in many cases did not fit the technical definition of war crimes (for example, inhumane acts against civilians who were not enemy nationals) and yet were unquestionably contrary to the dictates of the public conscience and general principles of law recognized by the community of nations'. In doing so, the Charter supplied elements that have remained central to concepts of crimes against humanity:

- *The crimes must target civilians.* In modern times, a range of humanitarian obligations in war, encompassing both combatants and noncombatants, is outlined in the Geneva Conventions of 1949. The Conventions themselves, like the Universal Declaration of Human Rights and the Genocide Convention, are part of the great wave of postwar rights-framing and institution-building that also gave birth to Nuremberg. Crimes against humanity are distinct from other categories in that they exclusively target civilians. An important issue here is whether the category includes only non-combatants who have never had an active military role; or whether it should also include the recently disarmed and neutralized. A core transformation in war, since the French Revolution but particularly since World War I, has been the advent of 'total war', in which mass populations are mobilized and administered for war-related production. Under such circumstances, distinctions between combatant and civilian are blurred. Accordingly, the understanding of 'civilian' in contemporary framings of crimes against humanity focuses on whether individuals pose a meaningful military threat *at the time they are targeted*. To cite the 1998 judgment of the International Criminal Tribunal for Rwanda (ICTR) in the case of Jean-Paul Akayesu: 'Members of the civilian population are people who are not taking any active part in the hostilities, including members of the armed forces who laid down their arms and those persons placed *hors de combat* by sickness, wounds, detention or any other cause.' Massacre and mistreatment of prisoners of war, such as those against

Soviet troops captured by the Nazis and Allied soldiers taken by the Japanese, may therefore constitute a crime against humanity, if they meet two further requirements:

- *The crimes must be widespread or systematic, and repeated.* By the time the Rome Statute of the International Criminal Court came into force in 1998, this had been codified in Article 7 (subparagraph 2(a)), which notes that an 'attack directed against any civilian population' must feature 'a course of conduct *involving the multiple commission of acts*' (emphasis added). The Rwanda tribunal (ICTR) has defined 'systematic' attacks as 'thoroughly organized and following a regular pattern on the basis of a common policy involving substantial public or private resources'. The systematic aspect also implies that crimes against humanity *are the product of a discernible policy* – a 'course of conduct' implemented by a state or quasi-state authority. In the Rome Statute, this finds expression with the reference to attacks '*directed* against' civilian populations.

- In all of this, it is implied that *the crimes must be intentionally committed.* The *mens rea* (mental element) of crimes against humanity must be demonstrated. The perpetrator must be shown to have been aware that an attack was occurring, would occur, or was highly likely to occur, and also that it was linked to a wider, systematic campaign against a civilian population. This *mens rea* component directly reflects similar provisions in most domestic legal systems.

International tribunals and the Rome Statute

The legal mechanisms developed to try accused perpetrators of crimes against humanity, genocide, and war crimes in the former Yugoslavia and Rwanda were ad hoc international tribunals. They were struck to deal with the events in question, and to look no further. A universal body did exist, the International Court of Justice (ICJ), established along with the League of Nations after World War I and incorporated into the United Nations structure after World War II. But the ICJ primarily adjudicated disputes between state parties, over boundaries, resource exploitation rights, and so on. It displayed a reluctance to intervene in the areas traditionally deemed under the 'sovereign' authority of the state. Not until February 2007 did the ICJ actually rule on a case involving alleged genocide and crimes against humanity – when Bosnia–Herzegovina accused Serbia, another state entity, of committing genocide against it during the war of Yugoslav succession (1992–5). While the ICJ established the significant precedent that states, not just individuals, can be authors of genocide, it rejected the Bosnian claim on the frankly dubious grounds that evidence did not demonstrate Yugoslavia's 'specific intent' to commit genocide.

What was needed was a systematization of the legal framework through a permanent institution which could issue indictments for genocide, crimes against humanity, war crimes, and crimes of aggression; supervise the detention and trial of accused perpetrators; and incarcerate those convicted of crimes. (The death penalty was ruled out from the start, an interesting demonstration of the way that a powerful prohibition regime against capital punishment has established itself globally, though still with notable holdouts such as China and the US.)

In 1994, the United Nations drafted a charter for the International Criminal Court, a legal body that would resemble the Yugoslavia tribunal, but be permanent and exercise universal jurisdiction. In July 1998, the text of the charter was finalized at a gathering of sixty-six countries in Rome, and by late 2007, 105 countries had formally joined the Court by ratifying it in domestic legislation, with dozens more who had signed but not yet ratified. A small handful of states refused to come aboard, most notably the United States (which signed but did not ratify the treaty), China, and Israel. These countries feared their national sovereignty would be undermined, though the ICC charter explicitly stated that the court would issue indictments only when national authorities manifestly failed, or were unable, to do so.

The Rome Statute's codification of 'crimes against humanity' is likely to serve as the legal benchmark for decades to come, and will be deployed frequently in these pages. The relevant section of the statute (see Box below) is more detailed than previous framings, but draws its scope and language largely from them. As Darryl Robinson observed, the ICC definition 'generally seems to reflect most of the positive developments identified in recent authorities. For example, the definition does not require any nexus to armed conflict, does not require proof of a discriminatory motive, and recognizes the crime of apartheid and forced disappearance as inhumane acts.'

CRIMES AGAINST HUMANITY: THE ROME STATUTE OF THE ICC

For the purpose of this Statute, 'crime against humanity' means any of the following acts when committed as part of a widespread or systematic attack directed against any civilian population, with knowledge of the attack: (a) Murder; (b) Extermination; (c) Enslavement; (d) Deportation or forcible transfer of population; (e) Imprisonment or other severe deprivation of physical liberty in violation of fundamental rules of international law; (f) Torture; (g) Rape, sexual slavery, enforced prostitution, forced pregnancy, enforced sterilization, or any other form of sexual violence of comparable gravity; (h) Persecution against any identifiable group or collectivity on political, racial, national, ethnic, cultural, religious, gender . . . or other grounds that are universally recognized as impermissible under international law . . . (i) Forced disappearance of persons; (j) The crime of apartheid; (k) Other inhumane acts of a similar character intentionally causing great suffering, or serious injury to body or to mental or physical health.

The court formally began operations in 2005, issuing its first indictments for crimes against humanity. At first exclusively, and still overwhelmingly, its subjects for prosecution have been drawn from African conflicts such as those in Sierra Leone, Liberia, and Darfur (a region of Sudan). This parallels the broader trend in national and international law of targeting former leaders of countries beyond 'the West' – most famously Augusto Pinochet of Chile and Yugoslavia's Slobodan Milosevic. A conceptual and practical leap will occur when a Western leader, present or former, is indicted for genocide or crimes against humanity, if one ever is.

Evolving understandings

If the core norms and framing of crimes against humanity were set down at Nuremberg in 1946–7, subsequent declarations – and legal proceedings, especially those of the 1990s-era international tribunals – have entrenched a number of other important aspects. Among those that will surface regularly in this book are:

- *Crimes against humanity are international in character, and subject to universal jurisdiction.* In the concise summary of the 'Principles of International Law Recognized in the Charter of the Nuremberg Tribunal and Judgment of the Tribunal', a declaration issued by the UN General Assembly in 1950: 'The fact that internal law does not impose a penalty for an act which constitutes a crime under international law does not relieve the person who committed the act from responsibility under international law.' The Rome Statute's 'Elements of Crimes' likewise stresses that 'crimes against humanity . . . are among the most serious crimes *of concern to the international community as a whole*' (emphasis added).

- *They may occur in war or peace* – or a context somewhere in between. The Nuremberg tribunal was preoccupied to the point of obsession with a need to frame Nazi atrocities as part of a campaign of 'aggressive war', designated as the highest crime under international law. This reflects the conviction of chief prosecutor Robert Jackson that 'crimes against humanity [were] ancillary to aggression'. Jackson believed that, under existing international law, such crimes as the 'program of extermination of Jews and destruction of the rights of minorities' could only be construed as subjects of 'international concern' because of their connection to a war of aggression. 'Unless we have a war connection as a basis' for prosecuting such crimes, Jackson argued, 'I would think we have no basis for dealing with atrocities.' The result, according to Gary Jonathan Bass, was that 'crimes against humanity got relatively short shrift' at Nuremberg.

This understanding carried over to the UN's 1950 declaration on 'Principles of International Law' derived from Nuremberg. It stressed that crimes against humanity – namely 'murder, extermination, enslavement, deportation . . . or persecution' – were necessarily 'done or . . . carried on in execution of or in connection with any crime against peace or any war crime'. Crimes against peace, in turn, included first and foremost 'planning, preparation, initiation or waging of a war of aggression or a war in violation of international treaties'.

Since the early postwar period, however, crimes against humanity have undergone a shift, reflecting at least some erosion of the state-sovereignty paradigm and the concept of 'aggression' that emerged from it. This seems traceable to the Universal Declaration of Human Rights (1948), and the assertion in the UN Genocide Convention of the same year that genocide could be committed 'in time of peace or war' (see chapter 2). The enormous humanitarian impetus established in the half-decade after World War II also gradually deepened, extending additional protections to vulnerable civilian populations, even when they were targeted domestically under claims of exercising legitimate state sovereignty. (See, for example, the discussions of torture in chapter 6 and apartheid in chapter 9.)

- *The crimes 'must be inhumane in nature and character, causing great suffering, or serious injury to body or to mental or physical health'.* This is the language of the seminal Akayesu judgment issued by the Rwanda genocide tribunal (ICTR) in 1998. The gravity of the concept of crimes against humanity – their universal application, and the universal jurisdiction that states hold to prosecute them, or to arrest suspects for prosecution by an international body – requires that the acts committed be of a grave nature. A suggestion here is that the damage inflicted by crimes against humanity must be felt in the long term, if not permanently. When the effects of physical or psychological harm last for years or decades – when they may last for centuries, as with dispossession and forced population transfer (chapter 3) – then the framing of crimes against humanity is more strongly supported. Murder, of course, is the most final destruction of all.

- *Crimes against humanity are committed by individuals.* The 'Elements of Crimes' of the Rome Statute is emphatic in declaring that crimes committed against the largest collective – humanity – 'warrant and entail individual criminal responsibility'. This represents the culmination of an international trend that arguably began with the Allied declaration of 1915, and the subsequent (abortive) legal proceedings against individual Ottoman Turk perpetrators of the Armenian genocide. The Nuremberg and Tokyo tribunals emphatically denied accused Nazis the opportunity to displace blame onto a broader political regime. The Genocide Convention likewise assigned responsibility exclusively to individuals, and all criminal prosecutions for genocide have been of individuals. Subsequent trials of Nazi war criminals – in the Soviet Union, France, Poland, Germany, Israel, and elsewhere – strengthened this trend, emphasizing perpetrators' individual responsibility and making it part of case law in many nations.

• *State agents are the primary, but not the only, perpetrators.* This is an especially important feature, given the shift away from conventional (international) wars of aggression toward *civil* wars, waged by opposed forces within a single state. Nonstate actors, such as guerrillas, paramilitaries, warlords, and ordinary individuals, may be key players. All of these contexts and actors are now bound by the strictures of 'crimes against humanity', and are equally liable to arrest and prosecution.

'Persecution' and 'other inhumane acts'

This book does not deal at chapter length with the crime against humanity of 'persecution'. This category has a rather special and nebulous character: as M. Cherif Bassiouni notes, it 'is neither a crime in the world's major legal systems, nor an international crime . . . *unless it is the basis for the commission of other crimes*' (my emphasis). Accordingly, persecution acts as an adjunct to the crimes against humanity enumerated in this volume. It relates to the *discriminatory intent* with which crimes and violations of human rights may be perpetrated, to the *widespread or systematic character* of the attack, and to the *identities* of its victims. Specifically, like the Genocide Convention, it emphasizes the vulnerability of civilians to be targeted on the basis of a claimed or imputed collective identity: 'political, racial, national, ethnic, cultural, religious, gender . . . or any other grounds that are

universally recognized as impermissible under international law'
(Article 7(1)(h) of the Rome Statute). This echoes and expands
upon the Genocide Convention's emphasis on the targeting of
human beings on the basis of 'national, ethnical [*sic*], racial, and
religious' identity. Specific strategies of persecution are not
enumerated: what is important is that they are '*intentional* and
severe', and result in a violation of 'fundamental rights' (the
'Elements of Crimes').

'Other inhumane acts' were likewise not defined beyond the
reference to 'inflict[ion] of great suffering, or serious injury to
body or to mental or physical health, by means of an inhumane
act'. The vagueness was deliberate, according to Amnesty
International: designed to ensure 'that new forms of crime
against humanity . . . will not escape international criminal
responsibility' in the future. 'Inhumane acts' were outlawed as
well by the 1949 Geneva Conventions. In their commentary on
that instrument, the International Committee of the Red Cross
(ICRC) stressed the importance of an open-ended definition:

> It is always dangerous to try to go into too much detail –
> especially in this domain. However much care were taken in
> establishing a list of all the various forms of infliction, one
> would never be able to catch up with the imagination of future
> torturers who wished to satisfy their bestial instincts; and the
> more specific and complete a list tries to be, the more restric-
> tive it becomes. The form of wording is flexible and, at the
> same time, precise.

This offers the opportunity to gradually expand the ambit of
crimes against humanity, by designating more actions as
'inhumane'. I return briefly to this theme in the Conclusion.

2

Genocide and extermination

In a strictly legal sense, genocide is not a 'crime against humanity' at all. It is the subject of its own international convention (the International Convention on the Prevention and Punishment of the Crime of Genocide, 1948). Recent judgments influential in shaping our understanding of both crimes against humanity and genocide, such as the Rwanda tribunal's Akayesu judgment of 1998, have stressed distinctions between the two concepts.

Yet genocide is often depicted as the 'crime of crimes'. And if the crime is not against human beings on a massive and systematic scale – therefore, in the contemporary understanding, a crime against all humanity – then what is? As early as 1949, legal scholar Joseph Dautricourt declared that 'genocide is also a crime against humanity and the wickedest of all'. Sixty years later, genocide scholar Martin Shaw likewise argues that 'in non-legal terms' the idea that 'genocide constitutes a crime against humanity . . . is self-evident'. Indeed, the preamble to the UN Convention acknowledges that 'at all periods of history genocide has inflicted great losses on *humanity*' (my emphasis). And while the drafting stage of the Genocide Convention featured spirited debate over whether genocide should be considered a crime against humanity, the position that the two are connected was tacitly acknowledged in the preamble to the Genocide Convention, which referred to the punishment at Nuremberg of acts 'analogous' to the crime of genocide.

On balance, it seems clear that excluding genocide from the range of crimes against humanity is a legalistic convenience. One can question the designation of genocide as the 'crime of crimes'. Very possibly, other human institutions – notably war, forced labor, and the global oppression of females – have been more destructive of human life than has genocide. But if it is not *sui generis*, there is no doubt that genocide is one of the supreme violations of human rights and physical integrity.

Genocide in history

Spirited debate swirls in comparative genocide studies around whether genocide should be considered essentially a *modern* phenomenon, linked to features of modernity such as technological development and modern concepts of race and ethnicity. The prevailing view, however, is that of the Genocide Convention, with its reference to 'all periods of history'. Genocide seems to reflect existential notions of self, community, and Other that may in fact extend deep into prehistory. Ronald Wright, in his book *A Short History of Progress*, suggests that the elimination of the Neanderthal population of Western Europe, about 40,000 years ago, may have been the first instance of genocidal extermination – or 'merely the first of which evidence survives'.

The religious texts of many civilizations, including Judeo-Christian ones, are full of sanguinary accounts of divinely ordained atrocities that look very much like genocide in its most exterminatory form. ('Spare them not; but slay both man and woman, infant and suckling, ox and sheep, camel and ass' 1 Samuel 15: 1–3; 'Slay utterly old and young, both maids and little children, and women' Ezekiel 9: 4–6.) Religious zealotry was also prominent in the New World genocides that followed the invasion and conquest of the Americas in the fifteenth and sixteenth centuries. Through a devastating combination of genocidal massacre, disease, malnutrition, and slave labor, perhaps ninety-five percent of the indigenous population of the Americas was wiped out following the arrival of Spanish, Portuguese, British, French, Danish, Dutch, and Russian forces. In some places, such as Hispaniola (present-day Haiti and the Dominican Republic), the obliteration of the native population – partly purposive, partly unexpected via infectious disease – was nearly total. The killing was rationalized by myths of civilizational superiority and the inevitably of indigenous peoples' disappearance. Sometimes the historical revisionism was so radical as to depict colonized territories as virgin lands, effectively free of indigenous populations at the time of Western 'discovery'. Remaining indigenous populations were either abandoned to destitution, or bombarded by propaganda demanding that they assimilate to the dominant culture: 'Kill the Indian, save the man' became a rallying cry of this more 'humane' approach. Only in the 1960s did dominant cultures in the West, spurred by indigenous peoples' activism (see Box overleaf), become more aware of the scale of destruction wrought, and the historical debt and obligation incurred.

'MY COUNTRY 'TIS OF THY PEOPLE YOU'RE DYING': BUFFY SAINTE-MARIE (1965)

Now that the longhouses breed superstition
You force us to send our toddlers away
To your schools where they're taught to despise their traditions.
You forbid them their languages, then further say
That American history really began
When Columbus set sail out of Europe, then stress
That the nation of leeches that conquered this land
Are the biggest and bravest and boldest and best.
And yet where in your history books is the tale
Of the genocide basic to this country's birth?
Of the preachers who lied, how the Bill of Rights failed?
How a nation of patriots returned to their earth? . . .

Hear how the bargain was made for the West:
With her shivering children in zero degrees,
Blankets for your land, so the treaties attest,
Oh well, blankets for land is a bargain indeed.
And the blankets were those Uncle Sam had collected
From smallpox-diseased dying soldiers that day.
And the tribes were wiped out and the history books censored,
A hundred years of your statesmen have felt it's better this way.
And yet a few of the conquered have somehow survived,
Their blood runs the redder though genes have paled.
From the Grand Canyon's caverns to craven sad hills
The wounded, the losers, the robbed sing their tale . . .

Figure 1 Cree-Canadian singer Buffy Sainte-Marie symbolized the resurgence of Native pride and identity in North America in the 1960s and '70s (see Box opposite). (Courtesy Buffy Sainte-Marie)

The twentieth century (1): Ottoman Turkey and Nazi Germany

Some of the power of the 'genocide as modernity' thesis derives from the sheer quantity and scale of genocides worldwide in the modern era. Of the literally dozens of twentieth-century cases that scholars have explored and sometimes rediscovered for modern audiences, three have acquired canonical status. The Ottoman campaign against Christian minorities of the Empire during World War I is standardly known as 'the Armenian genocide'. Some 1.5 million Armenians perished through direct murder, or on forced marches to the Syrian desert. The campaign, however, ranged beyond Armenians to target Assyrians in Mesopotamia (present-day Iraq), the ethnic Greeks of Anatolia, and the culturally distinct Pontian Greeks of the Black Sea Coast. In the crisis atmosphere of the war, all these Christian populations were viewed as traitorous and subversive. Waves of genocidal killing racked them well into the postwar era.

That postwar period was itself rent by economic and political upheavals – not least in Germany, which as a defeated power was subjected to economic sanctions to coerce it into accepting the punitive Versailles peace treaty (1919), then further tormented by hyperinflation. Conditions were propitious for the rise of extremist movements, none of which was more extreme than the Nazi (National Socialist) party. The Nazis were fueled by a pathological hatred of Jews, communists, homosexuals, and *Untermenschen* (subhumans) of all stripes. Nazi leader Adolf Hitler engineered the party's takeover of German politics in 1933, and set about isolating and persecuting the country's Jews and political dissidents, driving most of them out of the country or into concentration camps.

With the unleashing of World War II in September 1939, all constraints were removed from the genocidal impetus at the heart of Nazi ideology. Millions of Slavs, including more than three million captured Soviet prisoners of war, were murdered through execution, slave labor, and calculated starvation. Almost incomprehensible figures – in the tens of millions – have been cited for the death toll in the Soviet Union following the German invasion of mid 1941. Above all – at least in the Nazi hierarchy of priorities – the war was calamitous for the Jews of Nazi-occupied Europe. Murdered en masse by gunfire in the early months of the war on the Eastern Front ('the Holocaust of bullets', with 1.2 million killed), and consigned thereafter in their millions to the death camps constructed on Polish soil (most notoriously Auschwitz-Birkenau), the systematic destruction of the Jews came to represent the depths of Nazi evil more than any other atrocity. The comparative study of genocide, indeed, arose from earlier treatments and theorizing of what came to be called the Jewish Holocaust, or simply 'The Holocaust'.

The twentieth century (2): Rwanda

The intensity and ferocity of the hatred that fueled the Holocaust of the Jews has been matched by few events in history. One that deserves to be cited alongside it, however, is the genocide inflicted on minority Tutsis by majority Hutus in the small Central African country of Rwanda in 1994. Once again it was a war – this time a civil one – that created a crisis atmosphere and allowed extremist elements of an ethnic Hutu-dominated government in Rwanda to organize the extermination of the Tutsi minority, along with tens of thousands of dissident Hutus. Between April 6 1994 and the petering out of the genocide in July when the Tutsi-led Rwandan Patriotic Front (RPF) conquered most of the country, up to one million people were slaughtered, many by low-tech means like the iconic machete.

The killing proceeded at a faster pace than in the Jewish Holocaust, was accompanied by greater popular participation in the killing campaign, and displayed much the same discourse of virulent hatred and dehumanization as the Nazi precedent (for example, Tutsis were 'snakes' and 'cockroaches'). Moreover, while sharp accusations were made after World War II concerning the Allies' reluctance to devote resources to intervene directly in the Holocaust, in Rwanda international forces were actually *on the ground* throughout the genocide. A United Nations peacekeeping contingent was in place under Canadian general Roméo Dallaire, and when systematic mass killing erupted, foreign countries dispatched hundreds of highly trained soldiers to the scene. But their task was to evacuate resident whites from Rwanda. As for desperate Tutsis targeted for extermination, the message was 'Solve your problems yourselves', as one Belgian peacekeeper (captured on video) shouted as he decamped. The United States and other countries then engineered the downscaling of Dallaire's peacekeepers to what was, in more ways than one, a skeleton force. For the most part, Dallaire and his men could only watch helplessly as Tutsis were hunted down and hacked to pieces.

By common consensus, Rwanda marked the nadir of UN peacekeeping, and few other actors in the 'international community' emerged with reputations intact. The struggle to get to grips with genocide and put an end to it gained new force, leading to a new era in international human rights law. But the original impetus had been provided a half-century earlier, by an obscure lawyer and refugee from Nazi-occupied Europe.

Lemkin's word: genocide in international law

Genocide is one of the most powerful words in the English language: observe how international actors turn cartwheels to avoid having it applied to their own actions. Yet the term, which references atrocities extending thousands of years into the past, is a relatively recent invention. It was coined by Raphael Lemkin (1900–59), a Polish-Jewish jurist captivated, as a small child, by the violence inflicted on religious and ethnic minorities throughout history. He was also struck by the action of Soghomon Tehlirian, a young Armenian activist who in 1921 gunned down Talaat Pasha, one of the architects of the Ottoman Empire's genocide of Christian minorities during World War I. Tehlirian's action was deemed an act of vigilantism. But Talaat himself had been invulnerable prior to his assassination; no international law warranted his arrest. Wondered Lemkin to one of his law professors: 'It is a crime for Tehlirian to kill a man, but it is not a crime for his oppressor to kill more than a million?' In words that could serve as a kind of mantra for norm entrepreneurs the world over, Lemkin declared: '*This is most inconsistent.*'

During the 1930s, Lemkin experimented with terms such as 'barbarity' and 'vandalism' to capture the phenomenon of minority destruction, without fully persuading himself or others of their utility. When the Nazis invaded Poland in 1939, he fled to Sweden, east across the Soviet Union and then to North America, eventually arriving at Duke University, where he took up an academic post. At Duke, he finally settled on the word that would transform contemporary discourse: a neologism of the Greek *genos* (race, tribe) and the Latin-derived suffix *-cide* (killing). The suffix, especially in the wake of the Nazis' all-out campaign of physical extermination against European Jews, tended to enshrine in the public mind an equation of genocide with mass (indeed, total) killing. Lemkin's concept, however, was much broader. Genocide did not include killing only – or even primarily. Rather, the focus was on the dissolution and destruction of ethnic, religious, and other minority groups as such, which deprived human civilization of an essential part of its cultural heritage and diversity.

This emphasis on what some call 'cultural genocide' persisted

---

THE UN GENOCIDE CONVENTION (1948)

Article I: The Contracting Parties confirm that genocide, whether committed in time of peace or in time of war, is a crime under international law which they undertake to prevent and to punish.

Article II: In the present Convention, genocide means any of the following acts committed with intent to destroy, in whole or in part, a national, ethnical, racial or religious group, as such:

(a) Killing members of the group
(b) Causing serious bodily or mental harm to members of the group
(c) Deliberately inflicting on the group conditions of life calculated to bring about its physical destruction in whole or in part
(d) Imposing measures intended to prevent births within the group
(e) Forcibly transferring children of the group to another group.

---

to an extent in the international legislation that Lemkin almost singlehandedly steered through the nascent United Nations. His extraordinarily dedicated efforts resulted, in remarkably short order, in the UN Convention on the Prevention and Punishment of the Crime of Genocide (1948; see Box above).

It is striking to note, on first acquaintance with the Convention, that strictly speaking *no one need be killed at all for genocide to occur*. Acts aimed at dissolving and destroying the bonds of identity among group members – including preventing births within the group, or forcibly transferring the group's children – constitute genocide in themselves. This has led to important initiatives such as 'Bringing Them Home', a government-sponsored report issued in Australia in 1997. The report found that the institution of residential schools for Aboriginal children, together with other measures, had been forcibly imposed to supplant Aboriginal culture with that of the White majority. Therefore, the policies were genocidal. For the most part, however, genocide without mass killing has remained marginal in the debate, and in international law.

Confronting genocide today

Efforts to 'prevent and punish' genocides have ranged from institution-building, including the development and enforcement of human rights regimes, to state-led military interventions. The latter have usually been conducted by neighboring or nearby countries – those most directly affected by genocide's 'spillover' effects, notably international war and large-scale refugee flows. The Allied coalition in World War II eventually turned the tide of Nazi conquest in Europe, and brought an end to the Nazis' profligate genocidal practices. Since that time, India, inundated by ten million refugees, intervened in 1971 to suppress the Pakistani army's genocide in East Pakistan, now Bangladesh. Vietnam invaded Cambodia in 1978–9 and overthrew the genocidal Khmer Rouge regime; later in 1979, Tanzania expelled the military dictator Idi Amin from Uganda and ended his atrocious reign, only to replace it with another one presided over by Milton Obote.

In none of these post-World War II cases, however, were moral considerations paramount, or even especially prominent, in the equation. The era of 'humanitarian intervention' by military means awaited the end of the Cold War. The relaxation of superpower tensions allowed for options and initiatives that had earlier been foreclosed; but at the same time, the dissolution of the state-socialist world unleashed a slew of vicious civil conflicts. Perhaps none was more bloody than the breakup of post-Tito Yugoslavia. The war in the Balkans prompted little more than ineffectual posturing on the part of the European countries and the United States. A symbolic gesture, the creation of an international criminal tribunal (the ICTY), did nothing to dissuade the would-be conquerors – predominantly Serbs, but including Croats and Bosnian Muslims – from their course of genocidal massacre and 'ethnic cleansing' (see chapter 4). When UN-sponsored peacekeepers arrived, they were repeatedly humiliated and left almost defenseless in the wake of continued Serb aggression, culminating in the capture of the Srebrenica 'safe area' in July 1995. The result of that impotence – the Srebrenica massacre of some 8,000 Bosnian Muslim men and boys – galvanized the international community during a subsequent round of Serb 'cleansing', this time in the ethnic Albanian-dominated province of Kosovo, in southern Yugoslavia. When the Serbs launched their brutal crackdown against the Kosovar civilian population in March 1999, killing thousands and expelling hundreds of thousands to Albania and Macedonia, NATO dithered. It limited its military intervention to aerial bombing from 10,000 feet, killing civilians more often than Serb fighters. But combined with diplomatic pressure from Serbia's Russian ally, it proved enough to expel Serb forces from the province, end the killing – though revenge murders of remaining Serbs quickly followed – and bring the refugees home. It also paved the way for a more effective intervention several months later, in the tiny territory of East Timor at the eastern end of the Indonesian archipelago.

Indonesia had invaded East Timor – the western half of Timor was already part of Indonesia – following the precipitous departure of Portugal, the colonial power, in 1975. The campaign of conquest killed about a third of the population by mass executions, bombing, and above all starvation. Most of the surviving Timorese fled to remote mountain areas. For nearly twenty years, the world seemed uninterested. The Western powers, notably the US and UK, supported Indonesia's military ruler, General Suharto, as an anti-communist bulwark. But in 1991, Indonesian troops perpetrated a massacre in the capital, Dili, which was caught on film, arousing international condemnation. Two Timorese resistance leaders, Bishop Carlos Filipe

Ximenes Belo and José Ramos-Horta, were awarded the Nobel Peace Prize in 1996. And in 1998, with the Cold War long in recess, Suharto fell from power. His replacement, B. J. Habibie, offered the Timorese a vote on their future. Would they choose independence or continued association with Indonesia?

Timorese voted massively for independence. The Indonesian army, and the pro-Indonesian militias who had waged a campaign of murder and intimidation in the run-up to the plebiscite, responded as they always had – brutally, with a systematic campaign of murder and destruction. But this time, the conscience of the world was aroused. The Kosovo precedent – when NATO had claimed a right and responsibility to intervene to protect civilian life – was still fresh. So, too, were memories of the catastrophic inaction by the UN at Srebrenica, and before that in the Rwandan genocide of 1994. UN staff refused an order to evacuate their Dili headquarters. Tens of thousands took to the streets in neighboring Australia, where the Timorese solidarity movement was strongest, and in cities around the Western world.

In a remarkably short time – a matter of days – a tipping point was reached. Western states were forced to explain why they would *not* support military intervention in Timor to quell the atrocities, when they had so eloquently proclaimed an obligation to do so in Kosovo mere months before. Australia, shamed by demonstrators into overcoming its longstanding interest in placating Indonesia, announced it was willing to lead an intervention force, if the Indonesian government agreed. The Indonesians were persuaded to acquiesce by the firm threat of a cutoff in military aid by the Clinton administration – which was under its own acute moral pressure. Australian troops arrived, East Timor was placed under UN custodianship, and two years later it was granted the status of the world's newest independent state.

In all this, a new prominence was evident both for

humanitarian-inspired pressure on state actors, and for the organizations, networks, and individuals intent on applying it. The catalyzing and mobilizing role of nongovernmental solidarity organizations such as the East Timor Action Network (ETAN) was essential in the Timorese case. It has remained vital in the subsequent period of activism against genocide and related crimes against humanity.

The spark for a new generation of anti-genocide activists was the outbreak of genocide in Darfur, a large province of south-west Sudan. The genocide was ongoing at the time of writing. Eric Reeves, a professor of English at Smith College, achieved international prominence for his expert blogging on events in Darfur (www.sudanreeves.org). Branches of STAND (Students Taking Action Now – Darfur) blossomed on North American university campuses, launching a range of imaginative initiatives such as 'Picture a World without Genocide', in which students were encouraged to upload photographs of their Darfur actions and events. The images were then combined on a large banner unfurled at a major STAND demonstration in Washington.

STAND and others have also made artful use of seemingly unrelated events as a 'hook' for their anti-genocide activism. Chinese support for the Sudanese government, predicated on China's ambitions to secure overseas energy resources (Sudan is a major oil exporter), was difficult to oppose materially. China is after all a dictatorship, exerting tight controls over the domestic flow of information. A solution was found at the level of symbolism. China was eagerly declaring and promoting the norm of world peace through global sporting interaction, as symbolized by its hosting of the 2008 Olympics in Beijing. The slogan adopted for those games was 'One World, One Dream'. The dissonance between China's pacific rhetoric and its support for a genocidal regime created an arena for symbolic contestation. STAND launched a campaign to 'Bring the Olympic Dream to Darfur', which included an 'Olympic Torch Relay from Darfur to Beijing' paralleling the progression of the official torch. Pro-Darfur activists also sought to rebrand the world's pre-eminent sporting event as 'The Genocide Olympics'. The phrase was first deployed by the actor Mia Farrow and her son, in an op-ed piece written for *The Wall Street Journal*.

In this manner, movement activists were able to apply strategies of shaming and moral suasion. They appeared to have found at least a small soft spot in China's political armor. Much evidence suggests that existential considerations – honor, shame, humiliation – can be just as potent in state decisionmaking as traditional material factors. State policies can be confronted and contested symbolically by nongovernmental actors as effectively as, or more effectively than, states and intergovernmental organizations can apply economic, diplomatic, and military pressure.

However, while the activism surrounding Darfur was undeniably imaginative and impressive, it was an open question how effective it was. A reduction in killings in 2007 was claimed by many observers. But as with Iraq during the same period (see chapter 3), did this reflect constraints on the genocidal impetus, or merely an absence of available victims as large areas were 'ethnically cleansed'? The shaming strategies adopted toward China, at a particularly sensitive juncture, did seem to have captured Chinese attention and shifted the country's diplomatic position to a degree. But Sudan's core support for the genocidal Janjaweed militia was unsuppressed, and the authorities in Khartoum seemed to take pleasure in dancing a minuet with the international community: first accepting the dispatch of peacekeepers, then placing obstacles in their way; agreeing to broad rules of engagement and helicopter support for the peacekeepers, then stonewalling on implementation. Without a sense of crisis to foster international concern and consensus, it was essentially business as usual.

Understanding 'extermination'

It is not quite correct to say, as Darryl Robinson does, that the language of the crime of extermination in the Rome Statute of the ICC is 'borrowed from the Genocide Convention'. Rather, the Genocide Convention itself drew upon the framing of extermination in the charter of the Nuremberg tribunal (see chapter 1) to craft Article II(c) of the Genocide Convention. The drafters of the Rome Statute piggybacked, in turn, on Article II(c). The Statute's 'Elements of Crimes' declares that extermination must occur 'as part of a mass killing of members of a

---

'GENOCIDE' vs 'EXTERMINATION': CONVENTION ON THE PREVENTION AND PUNISHMENT OF THE CRIME OF GENOCIDE, ARTICLE II, 1948

In the present Convention, genocide means . . . deliberately inflicting on the group conditions of life calculated to bring about its physical destruction in whole or in part . . .

ROME STATUTE OF THE INTERNATIONAL CRIMINAL COURT (ICC), 1998

'Extermination' includes the intentional infliction of conditions of life, inter alia [among other things] the deprivation of access to food and medicine, calculated to bring about the destruction of part of a population . . .

---

civilian population', and includes killing 'by inflicting conditions of life calculated to bring about the destruction of part of a population' – the latter almost a direct lift from the Genocide Convention (see Box on p. 28).

The practical and philosophical crossover with the Genocide Convention is interesting, but also slightly awkward. Just as distinctions between genocide and crimes against humanity seem a legalistic convenience, so attempts to separate genocide and extermination seem casuistic. In 1996, for instance, the UN's International Law Commission noted that the inherently mass character of extermination meant that it was 'closely related to the crime of genocide'. But 'extermination' could also apply 'to situations that differ from those covered by the crime of genocide':

> Extermination covers situations in which a group of individuals who do not share any common characteristics are killed. It also applies to situations in which some members of a group are killed while others are spared.

As we have seen, however, genocide is by no means excluded where part of a targeted group is preserved from physical destruction, as the last quoted sentence implies. The essential international-legal instrument, the UN Genocide Convention of 1948, explicitly states that a group may be targeted for destruction 'in part', not only as an undifferentiated whole. The Appeals Chamber of the Yugoslav tribunal (ICTY), issuing its judgment in the case of Radislav Krstic's conviction for genocide at Srebrenica, established the precedent that the physical killing of a 'substantial' part of the group is sufficient to constitute genocide, and upheld the decision of the trial Chamber that 'the intent to kill the men (of military age) amounted to an intent to destroy a substantial part of the Bosnian Muslim group'.

We are thus left with the aspect that the crime of 'extermination' does not require that a clear group identity exist among its targets, or be imputed to them by the perpetrator. (The scope of the Genocide Convention, by contrast, is limited to the destruction of 'national, ethnical, racial, or religious groups'.) Perhaps this is of more practical than analytical interest. It suggests that prosecutors of the crime against humanity of extermination need not demonstrate genocidal intent, and a conviction generally lands a criminal behind bars for about the same period as would a finding of genocide.

My personal interest in the concept of 'extermination' pertains to its overlap with Article II(c) of the Genocide Convention. Both framings lend themselves to situations where specific genocidal intent may be hard to demonstrate, but where *constructive* intent can be shown. The perpetrators knew, or evidently should have known, that policies would have a destructive impact, even if that destruction was incidental to another purpose or motive. For example, a population may be consigned to slavery or forced labor with the purpose of extracting wealth from their labor-power. But if the population is exterminated in whole or in substantial part, by conditions of labor exploitation that are intentionally imposed – with consequences both foreseeable and actually observed – then the action constitutes a crime against humanity, whether one chooses to label it 'genocide' or 'extermination'.

Extermination, and its related article in the Genocide Convention, thus seem especially fruitful in cases where mass killing is *more indirect and/or institutionalized*. So far, the exploration of this potential in international case-law has been fleeting and frankly unimaginative. For example, 'extermination' rather than 'genocide' was preferred in the chargesheet for Mitar Vasiljevic before the Yugoslav tribunal – but only because instead of engaging in one-on-one killing, he had allegedly helped to lock dozens of Bosnian Muslims into a house, set it on fire, and provided illumination for others to shoot at anyone trying to escape. (Vasiljevic was in fact acquitted of the charge.)

This is indirect killing only in the most superficial sense. But the tribunals, and more recently the drafters of the Rome

Statute's 'Elements of Crimes', have declared their understanding that extermination can include 'deprivation of access to food and medicine', resulting in death through protracted debility. According to Machteld Boot, 'Other examples appearing in the case law of the Tribunals include imprisoning a large number of people and withholding from them the necessities of life, resulting in mass death, and introducing a deadly virus into a population and preventing medical care, which results in mass death.' Analyzing the legal dimension, the activist organization Christian Solidarity Worldwide has alleged that North Korean imprisonment practices (see chapter 5) may constitute extermination, since 'the direct killings and harsh conditions in the political prison camps have caused the deaths of a large number of the camp population, most probably resulting in the death of a significant part of the population constituting over 10,000 prisoners annually'.

Other atrocities that seem well suited to prosecution under extermination provisions are instances where mass death ensues from the intentional creation and perpetuation of famines. Cases cited in the genocide-studies literature include India under the British, Stalin's Soviet Union, China under Mao, and Ethiopia during the reign of the military regime known as the Dergue. In his seminal study of 'Famine Crimes in International Law', David Marcus acknowledges that such crimes, especially where they are both widespread *and* systematic, 'could be considered crimes of extermination' – noting that 'this crime has seen little jurisprudential development, making it ripe ground for rooting famine crimes'. This framing was echoed by the findings of the UN-supervised Truth and Reconciliation Commission for East Timor, in October 2005, that Indonesia had 'consciously decided to use starvation of East Timorese civilians as a weapon of war . . . The intentional imposition of conditions of life which could not sustain tens of thousands of East Timorese civilians amounted to extermination as a crime against humanity committed against the East Timorese population.'

Other crimes might usefully be drawn into the field of extermination practices. Denis Halliday was the UN Humanitarian Co-ordinator for Iraq during years in which UN-supervised economic sanctions were having a calamitous effect on the civilian population of the country. After resigning in protest at the humanitarian impact of the sanctions, he leveled a charge of genocide that echoed the extermination provisions of Article II(c) of the Genocide Convention. The Security Council, he declared, had not only committed crimes by bombing 'civilians and civilian infrastructure', but also, 'in an even more deadly, quiet and sustained manner of warfare', killed hundreds of thousands of people 'by the ongoing regime of comprehensive sanctions'. 'Whether it is de jure or de facto genocide,' Halliday stated, 'the semantics are irrelevant to those people of Iraq who have seen their children die, their parents die, and their own health and the health of most deteriorate into a state of physical malnutrition, a condition of near national depression and an environment of social collapse.'

At the outer reaches of this framework, one might deploy the concept of extermination to address the enormous human destruction caused by structural violence – poverty, hunger, the oppression of women, environmental despoliation, and other deeply embedded human institutions. Only in cases where ample empirical evidence exists, a causal chain is relatively short, and actors have ample opportunity to perceive the consequences of their actions, could we truly imagine a perpetrator being tried for extermination or complicity in genocide. One might envisage the head of a multinational corporation facing such charges for acts of gross human exploitation, environmental destruction, or negligence towards safety standards, something that would not be without precedent in national and international law. But 'extermination' and its related genocide provisions may serve better to generate public debate and activist mobilizations against

structural forms of violence. These are often far more exterminatory than conventional wars and genocides, but may be so
deeply embedded in our cultures as to be almost invisible – a
situation ready-made for 'norm entrepreneurs' to explore and
exploit.

3

Forced population transfer and 'ethnic cleansing'

> The perpetrator deported or forcibly transferred, without grounds permitted under international law, one or more persons to another State or location, by expulsion or other coercive acts . . .
>
> Rome Statute, 'Elements of Crimes'

The uprooting and displacement of populations is a phenomenon as old as human conflict. 'From the beginning of recorded history,' writes historian Norman Naimark, 'dominant nations have attacked and chased off their lands less powerful nations and groups they deemed subordinate and alien.'

Displacement often exists alongside, and as part and parcel of, campaigns of genocide and extermination (chapter 2). That is, in attacking a given civilian population, perpetrators often kill some and expel others, through terrorization into flight or systematic removal. The intent is to ensure that a population is expunged from a given territory, ideally (from the perpetrator's point of view) without the possibility of returning and re-establishing itself when the campaign has subsided. The long-term goal is 'an irreversible change of the demographic structure, creation of ethnically homogeneous regions, and achieving a more favourable position for a particular ethnic group in ensuing political negotiations based on the logic of division along ethnic lines'.

It was in the 1990s that the specific concept of 'ethnic cleansing' (in the Serbo-Croatian language, *etnicko ciscenje*) was first used in the Balkans to describe this phenomenon of forced displacement through terrorism, harassment, and violence. The Serbs seem to have devised and deployed the term, along with the first use of 'genocide' in the contemporary Balkans context, to describe the alleged treatment of Serbs by the ethnic Albanian majority in Kosovo province. Ironically, this was then used as a justification for the Serbs' 'defensive' ethnic cleansing of entire populations from territories they had inhabited for centuries – not least in Kosovo itself, in Spring 1999 (see chapter 2 and further discussion below).

Although an ancient practice, forced population transfer gained a new impetus in the modern era with the great wave of Western colonial expansion beginning in the fifteenth century. Long before the contemporary era of 'ethnic cleansing', in the eighteenth and nineteenth centuries, the United States had implemented 'removal' policies towards indigenous peoples; both the British and German colonists herded aboriginal populations into prison camps where they died en masse. Around the time they were doing so, however, 'ethnic cleansing' was also afflicting European peoples, from Scandinavia to the Balkans. The case of the dissolving Ottoman Empire in the nineteenth and early twentieth centuries has attracted special scholarly attention, not least because it conditioned so much of modern Turkish–Western relations (and the enduring polemics over the Armenian genocide). Beginning with the Greek uprising of the 1820s, successive Christian populations sought to establish themselves as independent, ethnically defined nations – and by the outbreak of World War I in 1914, they had largely succeeded, reducing Ottoman possessions in Europe to a sliver. The process was catastrophic not only for Ottoman Muslim settlers and colonists, but for the descendants of indigenous populations who had converted to Islam under Ottoman rule. In the war for Greek independence (1821–2), perhaps 25,000 Muslims died at Greek hands. Tens of thousands more Muslim casualties followed, and hundreds of thousands of their coreligionists were 'cleansed' from Balkan lands as Ottoman authority was revoked throughout the region. The Ottomans responded with massacres and forced expulsions of their own. In 1876, repression of the Bulgarian uprising prompted the English prime minister William Gladstone to denounce the atrocities. Gladstone's articulation of a 'moral sense of mankind at large' represents one of the earliest expressions of a nascent 'crimes against humanity' framework.

The targeting of Ottoman Christian minorities for genocide in World War I was described in chapter 2. A final convulsion occurred after the war, when Greek forces, under the authority of the punitive Treaty of Sèvres (never ratified), occupied coastal regions of present-day Turkey and then pushed deep into the Anatolian heartland. This mortal threat to the emerging post-Ottoman state spawned the rise of modern Turkish nationalism under Mestafa Kemal (Ataturk), who turned the tide against the Greek armies and pushed them back toward the coast, leaving scorched earth and shattered villages behind them. Infuriated by this wanton destruction, the Turks unleashed a new round of atrocities against ethnic Greeks, including those of the distant Pontian lands along the Black Sea coast. These 'cleansings' culminated in horrifying scenes as the port city of Smyrna (now Izmir) was put to the torch, and desperate refugees plunged into the waters in an attempt to reach French and British vessels moored offshore. In the wake of this paroxysm, Greek and Turkish authorities reached an agreement to 'exchange' populations – notably failing to consult the populations themselves. Roughly 1.5 million ethnic Greeks were expelled from Turkey, while half a million Muslims, mostly Greek-speaking 'Turks', moved in the other direction.

'Ethnic cleansing' and genocide

It is worth pausing, before considering the modern period of 'ethnic cleansing', to interrogate the term and explore its relationship with the concept and practice of genocide.

Generally speaking, 'ethnic cleansing' has come to be preferred over 'genocide' when perpetrators emphasize the forced expulsion of populations, with mass killing a subsidiary element. Only campaigns where populations are corralled rather than expelled, with the intention of concentrating and annihilating them, qualify as genocidal in popular parlance. Sometimes the discourse in media, political, and academic circles seems merely, and dubiously, euphemistic. The impact of the term 'genocide' is so great that 'ethnic cleansing' is seen as a more cautious, less inflammatory formulation. Among scholars of mass violence, reliance upon an 'ethnic cleansing' vocabulary tends to accompany a more restrictive framing of genocide, limited to major or full-scale campaigns of physical extermination. Such is the line of thinking advanced by Michael Mann in his book *The Dark Side of Democracy*. Mann contends that 'ethnic cleansing' – the forced conversion of territories from multi-ethnic to mono-ethnic ones – has usually taken 'quite mild' forms. Only a minority of cases constitute what he calls 'murderous cleansing'. This is contrasted, in turn, with 'genocide', which Mann defines along the lines of UN Convention, with minor alterations.

For many other scholars, however – including this one – there are significant risks to adopting and deploying the term 'ethnic cleansing'. First, one confronts the quandary that merely using this phrase, shorn of quotation marks (which I retain throughout this volume), subtly validates the discourse of perpetrators. After all, they view certain populations as contaminating a territory, and their own atrocious actions as 'cleansing' it. Do we court complicity when we echo the terminology of the 'cleansers'? (Note, by contrast, that no perpetrator describes his or her own actions as 'genocide' – unless persuaded to do so by a plea deal!)

Things are muddied further on the analytical level. The most widely accepted definition of genocide, that of the UN Genocide Convention, does not require the total physical killing of a group. It is sufficient to destroy it 'in whole or in part' – and not only by killing. The infliction of severe physical or psychological suffering on members of the group – Article II(b) of the Genocide Convention – would seem standard practice in virtually any widespread or systematic expulsion of populations. These 'cleansings' may likewise impede reproduction within the target group (Article II(d)) – for example, the sexes are systematically separated through detention and conscription (and/or killing) of males, alongside the forced expulsion (and/or sexual assault and forced impregnation) of females.

In his recent inquiry, *What Is Genocide?*, Martin Shaw argues that ethnic cleansing is in fact so intimately bound up with genocide that there is '*perverseness*' (his emphasis) in attempting to separate them: 'Cleansing language invariably oozes genocidal intent, resonating with the idea of destroying, if not murdering, the groups to whom it is applied.' I agree, and suggest that 'ethnic cleansing' should be viewed as a more limited and selective *form* of genocide, rather than a qualitatively different phenomenon.

Let us now return to the narrative, examining how 'ethnic cleansing' intersected with the worst war in history, and the evolution of this criminal practice since.

Totalitarianism and World War II

Ethnic cleansing in the twentieth century is closely associated with the century's best-studied 'totalitarian' regimes: the USSR and Nazi Germany. The Soviet purges of the 1930s, in which

Joseph Stalin sought to annihilate all opposition within the Communist Party and to cow the population at large, were referred to as *chistki*, 'or "cleansings", a word that applies to cleaning clothes or peeling vegetables' (Robert Thurston). For the Nazis, 'cleansing' was an integral part of their strategic vision for occupied Europe. Whole populations were to be moved around the map like chesspieces, with millions inevitably dying as a result, to realize the Nazi dream of *lebensraum* (living space).

During World War II, both the Nazis and the Soviets perfected their 'cleansing' strategies. For the Soviets, this was more tactical in nature, reflecting the deep invasion of the land and the paranoia of the Supreme Ruler. When Soviet armies at first crumbled in the face of the Nazi assault of June 1941, an alternative explanation to Stalin's incompetence had to be found. Guilt was assigned, as usual, to 'spies', 'traitors', and 'saboteurs'. True enough, certain populations (for example, those of Ukraine and the Baltic states) briefly welcomed the Nazis as liberators from the Soviet yoke. Others might have been tempted to do so if Nazi offensives had pushed further into the strategic, resource-rich regions of the Caucasus and Black Sea coast. Accordingly, it was the ethnically distinct populations of these territories who bore the brunt of Stalin's wartime 'cleansings'. A veritable who's who of national minorities – 'Crimean Tatars, Soviet Koreans, Finns, Volga Germans, Lamyks, Karachays, Chechens, Ingush, Balkars, Black Sea Greeks, and Meshketian Turks' – were accused of succoring the invader, or preparing to do so.

One case in particular, the 'cleansing' and large-scale destruction of the Chechen minority of the Caucasus, sowed seeds that would sprout into mass conflict decades later. Some 78,000 Chechens were killed in the process of relocating them to distant exile – and tens of thousands more died in the bleak Central Asian landscapes to which they were consigned. The experience seared a generation of Chechen survivors, who likened it to the great wave of killings and expulsions that accompanied czarist Russia's original expansion into their territories during the nineteenth century. When the Soviet Union collapsed, and an independent Russia dispatched troops to keep Chechnya from separating from the republic, Chechen resistance was astonishingly fierce and protracted. An initial Russian invasion was eventually defeated, and a second was battled to a standstill for several years, before Russian power succeeded in imposing a peace of the grave.

For the Nazis, Poland following the invasion of 1939 served as a paradigmatic case of forced population transfer. The country was rapidly partitioned and re-organized into a Germanized territory linked to the Reich (called the General Government), from which all Polish Slavs and Jews not working for the Nazis were expelled; and residual territories for colonization and 'settlement', in which Jews were locked up in ghettos, and Polish civilians were left to fend for themselves amidst conditions of severe privation. For the Jews, along with the Roma (Gypsies) and Soviet prisoners captured after the invasion of the USSR, the endpoint was the most exterminatory form of genocide, with millions killed by execution squads and in gas chambers. Millions of non-Jewish Poles died as well, as was fully intended in the Nazi scheme. In fact, Nazi planners anticipated that establishing German *lebensraum* in the East would inflict 20–30 million deaths, mostly Slavs 'cleansed' from fertile and productive territories and dumped in barren ones.

By the end of the war in 1944–5, the Nazis – and all ethnic Germans, whether involved in or removed from the war effort – had provoked considerable hatred and thirst for vengeance across occupied Europe. What came their way in the last few months of the conflict, and in its aftermath, were forced deportations that often matched the expulsions inflicted by the Nazis (and the Soviets) – both in their epic scale and in their murderous character. No one who examines the history of 'ethnic cleansing' can fail to be impressed by the tit-for-tat nature of so many such campaigns. Populations that have been expelled, dislocated, or undermined may wreak acts of vengeance that can exceed the crimes originally committed against them. Thus it was that the ethnic German populations of Central and Eastern Europe, 12–14 million people in all, fled in terror or were forcibly expelled. Some 2.1 million were killed outright, or died from privation en route. Some of these Germans had indeed agitated for union with the German Reich, and worked with the Nazi conquerors. But a great many, whatever their broad sympathies, had not. And like the Volga Germans deported by Stalin earlier in the war, many were never given the opportunity to choose an allegiance.

Bosnia in the 1990s

As a strategic project, 'ethnic cleansing' is built around borders: their establishment, expansion, consolidation, and defense. When examining the collapse of the Yugoslav federation into civil war and genocide in the 1990s, therefore, one is not surprised to find the worst violence concentrated at strategic points along the boundaries of the former Yugoslav republics. Eastern and north-western Bosnia were especially devastated. This was where Serb militias, with assistance from the regular (Serb-dominated) Yugoslav army, were best positioned and equipped to advance their project of constructing 'Greater Serbia'. They did so systematically, using methods that would be repeated in the 1999 campaign to 'cleanse' ethnic Albanians from Kosovo in southern Serbia. As summarized by the journalist Mark Danner, the procedure involved:

1. *Concentration.* Surround the area to be cleansed and after warning the resident Serbs – often they are urged to leave or

are at least told to mark their houses with white flags – intimidate the target population with artillery fire and arbitrary executions and then bring them out into the streets.

2. *Decapitation.* Execute political leaders and those capable of taking their places: lawyers, judges, public officials, writers, professors.

3. *Separation.* Divide women, children, and old men from men of 'fighting age' – sixteen to sixty years old.

4. *Evacuation.* Transport women, children, and old men to the border, expelling them into a neighboring territory or country.

5. *Liquidation.* Execute 'fighting age' men, dispose of bodies.

This is a succinct account of a typical 'ethnic cleansing' strategy. A mass-killing component generally features, although the selective targeting of males may be replaced by generalized killing through attrition, as with the Caucasian populations aboard Soviet trains. This murderous aspect, as we have seen, makes 'ethnic cleansing' difficult to separate, theoretically and practically, from genocide.

The most intensive period of 'cleansing' in Bosnia was the initial one, in 1992–3. However, another deluge descended in mid-1995. Bosnian Serb forces chose to strangle the 'safe areas' which had existed since 1993 under (largely symbolic) protection by UN peacekeepers. The result was the greatest massacre of the war, in the region surrounding the border city of Srebrenica (chapter 2). Only a month later, in another tit-for-tat 'cleansing', 150,000 Serbs were uprooted from the Croatian territory of Krajina, where ethnic Serbs predominated, and which had declared itself separate from independent Croatia. Expelled to Serb-controlled areas of Bosnia and to Serbia itself, the Krajina Serbs became the largest refugee population in Europe – a status they retain, over a decade after the Dayton peace agreements of November 1995 finally brought about a territorial settlement.

I witnessed the consequences of that settlement firsthand in 2007. Large expanses of territory in Bosnia and Herzegovina had been 'cleansed' of non-Serb populations – although a trickle of Bosnian Muslims had returned to their homes in Srebrenica and elsewhere, under European Union supervision. En route from the capital city, Sarajevo, to the commemoration ceremonies for the Srebrenica massacre at the village of Potocari (see figure 2), we passed through Republika Srpska, one of the two 'entities' that the Dayton Accords established as constituent parts of Bosnia and Herzegovina. Serb police were stationed at every turn-off along the highway – not threateningly, but vigilantly. They were there to ensure that the buses, filled mostly with Muslim relatives of Srebrenica victims, proceeded directly to the ceremony at Potocari, and returned with equal dispatch to 'their own' communities. Small boys at the roadside flashed us three-finger salutes, symbolizing the Christian trinity and Serb nationalism.

Republika Srpska was granted forty-nine percent of Bosnian territory in the Dayton agreement; the remaining fifty-one percent was allotted to a still-fractious Croat and Muslim confederation. By the time of my visit, the Bosnian Serbs had fully consolidated their hold on the strategic territories lying adjacent to the border with Serbia proper. The picture was much the same in Sarajevo. The city that I had first known as a backpacking teenager – when Bosnia was still part of Yugoslavia, and Sarajevo served as a model of interethnic co-existence – had passed through the crucible of the 1992–5 siege by Serb snipers and artillery. Away from the Muslim-dominated city center, Serbs governed and policed their own neighborhoods. When I tried to catch a bus to Belgrade, the Serbian capital, I discovered they even had their own bus station, in 'cleansed' and Serb-controlled territory.

'THEY ALL WERE OUR NEIGHBORS':
'ETHNIC CLEANSING' IN BOSNIA

We were forced to abandon our home on June 28 when our house was burned. There was 'ethnic cleansing' and my husband was taken to a detention camp. We left our house but not the village. We moved all the time because of the shelling, looking for shelter with our neighbors and children. We would hide in cellars.

[My house was burned at] about 4:00 a.m., before dawn. We weren't in our house; we were staying together in groups because we were afraid of the infantry . . . We weren't sleeping; we were all dressed because of the shelling – you had to be ready to go to the woods. My daughter asked for water and, when I went to get it, a man said that our house was burning. We left the house in which we were staying when the shooting ended and went to the woods. All night soldiers were walking through the village burning houses . . .

The army came to the village to take the men to detention centers. There was a lot of blood on the streets. They killed and tortured them. I saw it happen; they put the men together and called out names. Those called by name were taken to a barn, and all we could hear were gunshots . . . After the killing, the women took care of the bodies and identified them. The older men buried the bodies . . .

One day, a soldier came and told us to go away because we had no right to be there. He said there would be no Muslims in the area and that we should be ready to go by 10:00 a.m. or else the Red Berets and White Eagles [Serb paramilitary forces] would come and kill us. Soldiers of the 'Serbian Republic' told us to leave. They all were our neighbors. They just put on uniforms and acted as if they didn't know us.

> Account of 'S. S.,' described as 'a forty-year-old Muslim woman from Trnopolje'; in Helsinki Watch, *War Crimes in Bosnia-Hercegovina*, vol. 2 (New York: Human Rights Watch, 1993), pp. 57–9.

Figure 2 Bosnian Muslim women attending the annual memorial ceremony for victims of the July 1995 Srebrenica massacre, at the cemetery and memorial site built at the village of Potocari, Bosnia and Herzegovina. About 8,000 Muslim men and boys were massacred by Bosnian Serb paramilitary forces. (Adam Jones photo)

Iraq

Most of the literature on 'ethnic cleansing' has focused on the European context. Such forced population transfers are, however, a global phenomenon. The partitions of the Indian subcontinent and Palestine in 1947–8 (and these regions' regular outbursts of ethnic conflict since) offer object examples. Many African conflicts can also be conceptualized as 'ethnic cleansing' campaigns. For space reasons, a single example from the Middle East must stand for this broader set of non-European cases.

Like Yugoslavia, Iraq was cobbled together following World War I, constructed from *vilayets* (provinces) of the shattered Ottoman Empire. The populations grouped together in this artificial fashion included Sunni Muslims, Shi'a Muslims, and Kurds. As such, Iraq was particularly vulnerable to conflict and political breakdown when political actors mobilized along ethnic lines, in the absence of a dictatorial strongman capable of imposing 'order'.

Under Saddam Hussein, one of the twentieth century's most brutal rulers, both Shi'a and Kurds suffered grievously. Up to 200,000 Kurds were slaughtered in the Anfal Campaign of 1988, with hundreds of thousands of survivors expelled from their homeland in northern Iraq to locations further south, where they could be more easily surveilled by the dictator's security forces. As for the Shi'a, they rose up en masse following Iraq's defeat in the First Gulf War of 1991. While invading US forces stood by, Hussein crushed the uprisings and re-imposed his tyranny in the Shi'a-dominated south of the country.

Even Hussein's legions of dead, however, paled alongside the casualties produced by the joint US and British invasion mounted in March 2003. Security collapsed under the lackadaisical, undermanned occupying forces. Iraqis began to look to members of their own ethnic group for subsistence and security – and to view other groups as a mortal threat. For the Kurds of the north, their own proto-state already in operation, the issue mattered little. The exception was in oil-rich Kirkuk, outside the zone designated as part of Kurdish-controlled territory after the 1991 war. There, a low-level ethnic conflict between Kurds, Turkmen, and transplanted Sunnis was brewing at the time of writing. As for the Shi'a and Sunni, antipathies ran deeper as a result of Saddam Hussein's suppression of the Shi'a rebellion, and his open favoritism toward members of his own Sunni minority. One of the many misplaced decisions of the US occupation was to construct a new political order along primarily confessional (ethnoreligious) lines. With communal identities thus sharpened, open conflict was easier to provoke – and there were extremists on both sides eager to provoke it, along with the terrorist wild card of Al-Qa'eda in Iraq.

'Ethnic cleansing' was the result, on a scale rarely seen in recent decades. In February 2006, a Shi'a shrine in Samarra was bombed by Sunni or Al-Qa'eda militants. Over the rest of the year, entire neighborhoods of Baghdad and large swaths of the Iraqi countryside descended into chaos. Thousands of Sunnis were murdered by militias operating under the aegis of the Shi'a-dominated Ministry of the Interior, while thousands of Shi'a were killed by Sunni death squads and Al-Qa'eda's suicide bombers. By late 2007, a staggering four million Iraqis had fled or been forcibly displaced – roughly half of them internally displaced within Iraq, and half seeking refuge in other Arab countries. For the internally displaced, refuge was usually sought among co-ethnics, so that a decline in civilian killings in the latter half of 2007 probably reflected the fact that the 'cleansing' of ethnically mixed communities was largely complete. By that point, credible estimates of the war's death toll ranged as high as one million.

The legacy of 'cleansing' and processes of reconciliation

Forced removal and accompanying dispossession spawn *irredentism*: the political expression of the conviction that your own claim to territories from which you or your ancestors were expelled outweighs any claim of the present-day inhabitants. Most irredentist projects are stymied by geopolitical realities: expellees and their descendants have no practical means to reassert their presence. What remains is an abiding bitterness. 'Many of the ethnically cleansed and their descendants retain a visceral anger and mistrust toward the perpetrators of expulsion and *their* offspring', writes Benjamin Lieberman. 'Decades after ethnic cleansing, a sense of victimization remains a core element of their identity. The sense of victimization extends even to diaspora communities whose members have moved far away . . . '

Poverty, marginalization, and alienation remain the norm for many of the forcibly displaced, and the generations who follow them. Indigenous populations systematically uprooted from their lands in the Americas, Africa, and Australasia are today their countries' poorest and shortest-lived minorities. The descendants of Palestinians forced out of Israel are scattered in a diaspora around the world; their alienation from native territories fuels nationalism, and sometimes terrorism, among new generations. The expulsion of Iraqi Kurds from Kirkuk province under the Saddam Hussein regime spawns, today, clashes between Kurds seeking to restake a claim to the oil-rich region, and Sunni Muslims and Turkmen seeking to defend their own claims, whether legitimately or illegitimately established.

Something more nebulous is stored up for a post-cleansing age: a residue of melancholy and absence; a cultural deficit. The Great Plains of the United States 'cleansed' of their native populations; the cosmopolitan villages of Thrace, the Aegean coast, and Anatolia, shattered by warring visions of 'Greece for the Greeks' and 'Turkey for the Turks'; the once ethnically mixed neighborhoods of Sarajevo, now divided into rigid cantons . . . Where once a stimulating conversation reigned, in 'cleansed' territories there reverberates only the monologue of the ethnic hegemon. In this sense, the crime against humanity of forced displacement and 'ethnic cleansing' manifestly *is* a crime against human civilization, and the diversity and communal complexity that compose it.

At times, especially when a generation or more has passed, processes of reconciliation may begin. An attempt may be made to build new bicommunal or multicommunal institutions – political bodies, security forces, and the like. Media outlets and government officials may seek to promote an atmosphere of reconciliation and overcoming of ethnic differences. Local initiatives may serve as test cases that can then be expanded in 'inkblot' fashion.

In divided Mostar in Bosnia, for example – a city whose streets and buildings were contested so fiercely by Croats, Serbs, and Muslims during the wars of the 1990s that many of them still lie in ruins – one scarred hulk has come to serve as a symbol of co-existence, if not full reconciliation. The façade of the Mostar Gymnasium (prep school), which stood on the front lines of the urban warfare of the 1990s, was ravaged by bullets and shellfire. More than a decade later, however, attempts were underway to bring together students from the two principal communities, Croats and Muslims – albeit in separate classes with separate curricula. Richard Medic, a representative of the Organization for Security and Cooperation in Europe (OSCE) which promoted the initiative, admitted that 'there was some fierce resistance initially, even [over] the proposed name of the reunified school . . . I spun, lobbied, cajoled, and begged for two years before that resistance yielded. It started with the kids, of course, and then the teachers and parents. But I really considered my job done once the more hard-line politicians started attending poetry readings at the reunified school.' Students mingled through sports, extracurricular activities, and adolescent flirtations. Whether these tentative expressions would blossom into a genuinely unified city, contributing to a newly multicultural tapestry in the lands of the former Yugoslavia, was highly uncertain. But it was not, perhaps, a goal out of reach for the 'norm entrepreneurs' who seek to heal dislocated and divided societies.

4

Slavery and human trafficking

Introduction

The Rome Statute defines enslavement as 'the exercise of any or all of the powers attaching to the right of ownership over a person'. Slavery's consigning of human beings to mere property 'deprives people of their most basic recognition as human beings'. It reduces them to the status of cattle, which is the root of the term *chattel* slavery – and indeed, slavery may have begun as an extension of the domestication of animals.

Until relatively recent times – say, the early nineteenth century – slavery's erosion seemed an unlikely prospect. Slaving institutions were deeply entrenched in societies worldwide. The Atlantic slave trade, aimed at exploiting the riches of the New World, was booming. The story of how slavery moved from the center to the margins of the global economy is one of extraordinary and constructive human effort. But it is also a testament to how atrocious institutions are more easily accepted as such when substitutes are readily available. If slavery as a global economic system and legal practice is a thing of the past, 'slavery-like practices' endure – to use the term deployed in a 1956 United Nations instrument drafted to confront them. They include human trafficking, which in international law is closely associated with the sexual exploitation of women and girls. This chapter will touch on all these themes.

Slavery as mass atrocity

The ubiquity of slavery throughout history has often been cited to excuse the destruction wreaked by particular slavery institutions. But the nature, and especially the murderousness, of slavery have varied dramatically in different historical contexts. On one hand, we find the consigning of the children and women of a conquered group to slavery, usually after the 'battle age' male population has been put to the sword. In patriarchal and patrilineal societies, women and children were more easily absorbed into the clan or tribe. What began as forced labor and concubinage often evolved into something resembling the 'normal' subordinate condition of children and women under patriarchy. They might eventually receive manumission (freedom) from slavery – a possibility also for men with skills who could be put to work more usefully than they could be put to death. Such slavery institutions were common across Africa, indigenous empires in the Americas, the Ottoman Empire, and the great 'Silk Road' trading route of the premodern period. Though often targeting the survivors of exterminatory campaigns, these institutions were usually not, in themselves, exterminatory. Slaves were booty – too valuable a commodity to destroy casually.

At the other extreme, we find slavery as genocide. The early record of the rise and decline of empires is replete with tales of entire populations being uprooted and scattered by slavery – and of slaves being worked to death as chattels. Such practices were sometimes part of nineteenth-century colonial regimes, as in German South West Africa and some parts of the Americas. There is a direct line of descent from colonial practices to the Stalinist labor camps in the Siberian gold fields, and Nazi slave-labor camps such as Auschwitz III-Monowitz and Mauthausen (these are discussed as cases of arbitrary imprisonment in chapter 5). Genocidal slavery has also appeared in unexpected places. In his study *Slavery and Social Death*, for example, Orlando Patterson writes that '*nothing in the annals of slavery . . .* can match the Indians of the US northwest coast for the number of excuses a master had for killing his slaves and the sheer sadism with which he destroyed them' (emphasis added).

Atlantic slavery, a system of triangular trade (moving slaves, colonial commodities, and European manufactured goods) that extended over much of the world from the fifteenth to the nineteenth centuries, similarly varied significantly across its enormous length and breadth. On balance, though, the Atlantic system 'was a conveyor belt to early death'. Even where survival rates on the plantations were relatively high, as in the southern US, the mortality rates for slaves en route from the African interior to West African ports, then across the ocean in slave ships such as the *Brookes* (figure 3), were devastating. Perhaps fifty percent of those originally taken captive in Africa did not survive to reach the New World.

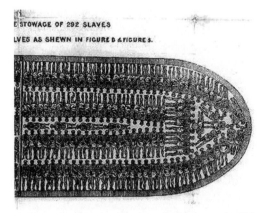

Figure 3 Detail of the famous diagram of Africans packed like sardines into the hold of the slave ship *Brookes*. The image was distributed around much of the world from the early 19th century as a vivid exemplar of slavery's horrors.

In many cases, the high mortality rate continued when slaves were sold and put to hard labor. A brutal 'seasoning' process killed tens if not hundreds of thousands. Working conditions were characterized by long hours of intensive labor, often in debilitating heat, with poor rations and little access to medical care. They produced a wastage so immense that in Haiti, for instance, when the great slave rebellion of 1791 erupted, most of the hundreds of thousands of slaves in the colony had been born in Africa. It proved cheaper to import fresh slaves than to devote the necessary resources to ensuring the subsistence and reproduction of those already there. The strategy was 'to wear [slaves] out before they became useless, and unable to do service; and then, to buy new ones, to fill up their places', as one plantation owner phrased it.

Few would guess that Haiti, one of the world's poorest countries, was in the eighteenth century one of the wealthiest places on earth – measured by the riches wrung from its soil by West African slaves working under French masters. It was the jewel in France's colonial crown, and the revolution that shook it from 1791 to 1804 was a major world-historical event. The revolt – the largest slave rebellion in history, and the most successful one – caused tens of thousands of deaths in unalloyed race wars and epidemics of tropical disease. It undermined French power in the Caribbean and North America; and by prompting the French revolutionary regime in Paris to end slavery everywhere in the French realm, then by establishing the world's first independent black republic, it shook Atlantic slavery to its foundations.

The Haitian Revolution was both a galvanizing and a catalyzing event. In 1807, only three years after Haitian independence was achieved, the British government banned the slave trade in the British Empire (though not chattel slavery as such, until the passage of the Abolition of Slavery Act in 1833). By the time of the Haitian events, however, religious and

ENSLAVED: OLAUDAH EQUIANO

When I looked round the ship . . . and saw a large furnace or copper boiling and a multitude of black people, of every description, chained together, every one of their countenances expressing dejection and sorrow, I no longer doubted of my fate; and, quite overpowered with horror and anguish, I fell motionless on the deck, and fainted . . . I was soon put down under the decks, and there I received such a salutation in my nostrils as I had never experienced in my life: so that, with the loathsomeness of the stench, and with my crying together, I became so sick and low that I was not able to eat, nor had I the least desire to taste any thing. I now wished for the last friend, death, to relieve me . . . The closeness of the place, and the heat of the climate, added to the number in the ship, being so crowded that each had scarcely room to turn himself, almost suffocated us. This produced copious perspirations, so that the air soon became unfit for respiration, from a variety of loathsome smells, and brought on a sickness among the slaves, of which many died . . . This deplorable situation was again aggravated by the galling of the chains, now become insupportable; and the filth of necessary tubs [of human waste], into which the children often fell, and were almost suffocated. The shrieks of the women, and the groans of the dying, rendered it a scene of horror almost inconceivable.

Olaudah Equiano, *The Interesting Narrative of the Life of Olaudah Equiano, or Gustavus Vassa, The African, Written By Himself* (1814)

working-class activism to suppress slavery had been underway in Britain and France for decades, and was taking hold in the United States as well. The movement employed sophisticated strategies of communication and publicity which still serve as models of activist innovation. It helped to disseminate vivid first-hand testimonies by former slaves, such as Oloudah Equiano (see Box above). One of its masterstrokes was to circulate an engraved schematic view of the slave ship *Brookes* (see figure 3, p. 59), showing slaves densely packed around the ship's hold. The image 'seemed to make an instantaneous impression of horror upon all who saw it', noted anti-slavery leader Thomas Clarkson. In Adam Hochschild's summation: 'precise, understated, and eloquent in its starkness, it remains one of the most widely reproduced political graphics of all time.'

The abolitionist movement was unprecedented, and may still be unmatched, in demonstrating the power of morally informed action to influence human affairs. According to international relations scholar Ethan Nadelmann, 'No other international prohibition regime so powerfully confirms the potential of humanitarian and similar moral concerns to shape global norms as does the regime against slavery and the slave trade.' From a world in which the trade was 'legal and commonplace', slavery was increasingly anathematized – and finally eliminated as an international institution. (It took the Civil War to end slavery in the United States, in 1865, but the institution lingered in Cuba and Brazil until the 1880s, and was not formally banned in Nigeria until 1936.) As well, the moral legitimacy of the anti-slavery struggle could be grafted onto campaigns to advance the rights of other subordinated peoples. 'If slaves should have rights, why not women? If the brutal working conditions of slavery should be outlawed, why not those in British factories?' Moral entrepreneurs have always used such techniques of 'norm grafting' to try to bolster support for new causes by drawing on the legitimacy of well-established and widely respected precedents.

Coerced labor after slavery

The dramatic transformation that the anti-slavery movement engineered should not overshadow the distinctive features that enabled slavery's suppression. Relying as it did upon an internationally sanctioned trade, slavery was relatively vulnerable to prohibition, monitoring, and policing. (It was much harder to hide slaves in ships' holds than, say, illegal drugs – let alone to maintain secrecy once slaves had been delivered clandestinely to their destinations.) Also, the evolution of the anti-slavery drive was gradual enough that slavers, plantation owners, and governments alike were able to construct alternatives that allowed them, in many cases, to adapt and thus perpetuate coercive labor exploitation, combined with political disenfranchisement. These systems often prevailed until the collapse of colonial systems in the mid-twentieth century, and regularly recur in the record of international labor practices today.

The strategy adopted in the United States was later dubbed 'Jim Crow'. Following the brief, thrilling flowering of Reconstruction – in which the post-Civil War South witnessed the rise of an African-American political and entrepreneurial class – white elites and workers alike mounted a reactionary attack against black aspirations. Literacy and property requirements, or wholly arbitrary measures, were used to excise southern black representation from electoral politics and effectively deny them the vote. The original promise of 'fifty acres and a mule' for freed slaves was replaced by sharecropping on white-owned plantations – that is, providing agricultural labor in return for the right to farm and settle on a sliver of land. The advantage for the plantation owner was that the newly 'free' laborer did not have to be fed, clothed, and housed year-round, but was nonetheless at the ready, to be called upon when needed.

Similar arrangements were imposed elsewhere in the Americas, along with the development of two institutions – *corvée* (forced labor) and debt peonage – dating from the Spanish colonial period. Forced labor meant that laborers could be drafted for infrastructural projects; debt peonage, which trapped laborers in unending cycles of debt, guaranteed a steady flow of labor to the plantations. There, workers could expect to be paid the merest pittance, and were forced to spend it in company shops – leading them to rack up ever greater debt, and incur a legal obligation to return in subsequent seasons to 'work it off'. Measures against 'vagrants' – those unable to demonstrate attachment and employment – were another means of disciplining post-slavery labor forces in the Americas.

From roughly the 1880s through the 1920s, forced labor was an essential feature of colonial practice elsewhere in the world. Belgian rapacity in Africa, for example, is legendary. King Leopold of Belgium (1835–1909) established as his personal fief an immense territory in the Congo (today's Democratic Republic of Congo). Millions of laborers died to produce the gold, ivory, and rubber that fed Leopold's hunger for power and wealth. They effectively worked as slaves – indeed, especially brutally treated slaves – who, if they survived their period of enslavement, often returned to their villages only to die there.

The depredations of Leopold's henchmen in the Congo gave rise to one of the very first international protest movements: the Congo Reform Association. It was led by a few well-known public figures (including the writers Sir Arthur Conan Doyle, of Sherlock Holmes fame, and Joseph Conrad, whose novella *Heart of Darkness* addressed the horrors of the Belgian Congo), and attracted the passionate interest of millions of ordinary citizens, especially members of trade unions and religious societies. 'Utilizing modern means of communication, the Association spread across the European continent and to North America, dispatched observers to the Congo and published their findings. All of this placed increased pressure on King Leopold to expose his territory to outside oversight.' Eventually he did, allowing investigative commissions and finally surrendering control of his fief to the Belgian parliament.

In 1926, the League of Nations passed the Convention on

Slavery, Servitude, Forced Labor and Similar Institutions and Practices. Four years later, the Forced Labor Convention banned most forced-labor practices (with an exemption allowed for the exploitation of males aged eighteen to forty-five – reflecting states' fears that the convention could be used to undermine their military conscription policies). Noble declarations, however, were no impediment to the resurgence of genocidal slavery and forced labor under German and Japanese occupation regimes during World War II. In the 'work camps' sponsored by the Nazis, the *purpose* was to work the inmates, at least Jewish ones, to death. No other conclusion was possible in the face of the systematic atrocities inflicted, and the abysmal standards of safety, shelter, nutrition, and medical care. In their occupation zone in the Pacific, the Japanese supervised the grotesquely misnamed 'Greater Asian Co-Prosperity Sphere', in which Chinese and Korean laborers, in particular, were exposed to horrors of enslavement that rivaled the Nazis'.

In the Soviet Union, the Gulag system of incarceration and forced labor served as a template for the vast Chinese prison system and the slavelike conditions – and labor exploitation – to which inmates were exposed. Both differed from formal slavery, but the difference was academic to the architects of the Stalinist 'Five Year Plans' or Mao Zedong's 'Great Leap Forward', and to their victims. All of these cases are discussed in greater detail later in this book, under the rubric of imprisonment as part of a widespread or systematic attack on a civilian population (chapter 5). Though rarely classed as 'slavery' by scholars of the subject, the dimension of labor exploitation that underpins these penal regimes at least *echoes* slavery – indeed, slavery in its most atrocious form.

Nor, in the Chinese case, is this a vestige of the Maoist past. Prison labor is still heavily exploited today to produce manu-factured goods for export. The policies have spawned initiatives in the US Congress to isolate and ban prison-produced goods from China. Ironically, the use of prison labor for minimal remuneration is widespread in the US itself: 'tens of thousands of prisoners labor for little or no pay as the work force that runs prisons . . . In some Southern states, like Texas and Louisiana, unpaid prisoners toil in the fields of former slave plantations just as chattel slaves did 150 years ago.'

Moreover, the highly globalized form of twenty-first-century capitalism has left important niches in the continuum of coercive labor practices, including slavery. It is tempting to see the plantations of old simply shifted 'offshore' to the lands of the newly enslaved. The laborers on plantations, or in sweatshops and *maquiladoras* – how different is their fate from that of the eighteenth- or nineteenth-century slave? They toil often under physically harsh conditions, for long stretches, under vigilant and sometimes punitive oversight, for a pittance that in some cases is promptly claimed back by their employers/exploiters as 'rent', or via payment in scrip valid only for purchases in company stores.

It may be argued that there is a qualitative difference between this type of hyperexploited labor and the slavery of past ages. A voluntaristic and contractual element generally exists, however constrained and coercive. Such hard labor may, by design, be the only way for exploited populations to access the cash economy. Not for nothing does the phrase 'wage slavery' resonate. But the period of 'slavery' or quasi-slavery, though it may be regularized, is not legally or physically compulsory. And it may also be actively sought. In the Pearl River Delta region of southern China, for example – the so-called 'sweatshop of the world' – highly exploited labor is seen as a step up, if not for the worker then for his or her descendants. Tens of millions of younger rural residents seek paid employment in the city as an alternative to the torpor and patriarchal backwardness of the countryside.

What about slavery as such? Though banished from the

international economy in anything like its former manifestation, it has not disappeared. Nongovernmental organizations offer widely varying estimates of the number of slaves today – from 2.7 million (the Anti-Slavery Society) to ten times that (Free the Slaves). In part to keep the numbers impressive, it seems that slavery is increasingly being blended in these campaigns with the separate phenomenon of human trafficking. Chattel slavery itself has been reduced to a twilight existence in a few marginal outposts. In the north-west African country of Mauritania, for example, legal slavery 'existed for hundreds of years'. Only in 1981 was it formally outlawed, 'but no one has ever been prosecuted for it and no law created a punishment' – until 2007, when the Mauritanian legislature 'unanimously adopted a law . . . promising prison time for people who keep slaves – a monumental step in the push to eliminate the long-standing practice.'

Human trafficking and smuggling

> It is also understood that the conduct described in this [enslavement] element includes trafficking in persons, in particular women and children.
>
> Rome Statute, 'Elements of Crimes'

Definitions of human trafficking vary greatly, sometimes confusingly. Most, however, emphasize that *deception* is generally involved – particularly early in the trafficking process, to snare a victim; and *coercion* usually follows, including violence and threats. Human trafficking can be distinguished from human *smuggling*, in which a would-be migrant (almost always poor) seeks or is convinced to accept the services of a contractor who will deliver him or her to a destination, almost always in the rich world or en route to it.

In practice, distinctions between trafficking and smuggling are harder to draw. There is often a heavy element of deception in human smuggling; many individuals believe they are being smuggled, only to discover that at their destination they are confined or otherwise restricted, and underpaid or unpaid. Smuggling as such likely kills and injures many more people than does trafficking – think of the thousands of African would-be migrants who drown every year, attempting to reach Western European shores. Yet it is trafficking, not smuggling, that has entrenched itself more vividly in the public conscious-ness, partly because of the apparent absence of a voluntary element, and partly owing to the fact that trafficking has come to be closely associated with the victimization of women and children. These are traditionally viewed as the most vulnerable groups, and their plight typically arouses the greatest empathy.

While falling short of chattel slavery, human trafficking and smuggling are the subject of anti-slavery provisions – or rather, those against 'slavery-like practices', as the relevant 1956 legal instrument defined them. The Rome Statute of the International Criminal Court, for example, states its 'under-standing' that slavery 'may, in some circumstances, include exacting forced labor or otherwise reducing a person to a servile status'. Likewise, the Statute declares that trafficking in human beings, which has aroused the greatest international consterna-tion over the past two decades, and has probably been the subject of as much governmental and nongovernmental atten-tion as any other humanitarian issue, may constitute enslave-ment, 'in particular [when] women and children' are targeted ('Elements of Crimes', Article 7(1)(g)-3).

The major networks of trafficking and smuggling worldwide are broadly familiar from the media reports of recent years. They include North and West Africa, Eastern Europe, and the Balkans to Southern and Western Europe; South and South-East Asia to the Persian Gulf and Japan; and Latin America (especially

A SURVIVOR'S STORY: EMILIE

Emilie arrived in the US at the age of 17 from Cameroon. She was accompanied by her 13-year-old brother. Her trafficker was her half-sister, related to her and her brother through a common father . . . Emilie had thought she would eventually come to the US for college anyway, but her sister convinced her parents to let Emilie and her brother come with her to the US so that they could attend American schools at a younger age.

Emilie's trafficker arranged the papers for her and her brother, claiming that they were actually younger than they were: 12 and 9 respectively. When they arrived in the US they found themselves put to work for several people in the sister's house – cooking meals and hand-washing clothes from 4 or 5 in the morning until late at night . . . The trafficker wrote letters home to Emilie's parents claiming that they were attending school and that everything was going very well. The reality, however, was that Emilie and her brother had been sustaining severe, regular whippings in the living room in front of the other occupants of the house. Often, Emilie had bruises and cuts on her face and head. Once the trafficker held her down on the floor and sat on her stomach until she could not breathe.

Emilie and her brother worked long hours with very little food and were beaten if the trafficker suspected that they had eaten without permission or been insubordinate in other ways. If Emilie was allowed to leave the house, it was only to buy groceries at a supermarket fifteen minutes away by car. She was forced to run or walk quickly with the groceries because the trafficker would time her. If her arrival exceeded this time limit, the result was a beating. She was too frightened to talk to anybody because her trafficker had told her that 'If you talk to anybody, they'll put you in jail'.

Emilie eventually sought help after reading an article about another Cameroonian girl in Washington DC who had experienced similar abuse . . . It was through reading about the girl that she summoned the courage to go to a neighbor's house to call the police.

Testimony compiled by Endabuse.org,
www.endabuse.org/programs/immigrant/files/PaintoPower.pdf

Mexico) and the Caribbean to the United States. As China has opened to the outside world in the last decade, so has the outflow of undocumented Chinese migrants increased. They have arrived in growing numbers in Europe and North America; after Mexicans, they likely represent the most numerous trafficked and smuggled population in the US.

Nor should one overlook the dense networks for *internal* trafficking (smuggling, usually conducted across national boundaries, is less relevant here). In Brazil, for example, labor agents known as *gatos* (cats) tour slums offering alcohol and wads of cash to men who will accompany them into the country's sprawling interior. Once there, the booze and promises wear off; the men are consigned to enormous *fazendas* (ranches), and 'forced to work without pay from sunrise to sunset under inhumane conditions. Those who refuse to follow orders are beaten and tortured; those who demand payment or attempt to flee are killed, their bodies mutilated and dumped in unmarked graves.'

A constant of human trafficking and smuggling, and perhaps the reason it has proved so difficult to confront, is its high degree of integration with above-ground economic patterns and processes. Hegemonic conceptions of 'globalization' emphasize its free-market dimension. In fact, however, one of the two underpinnings of a functioning free market is absent: while capital moves relatively freely, labor migration is tightly restricted. Smuggled and trafficked labor responds to this market deformation. Moreover, it has become integral to the operation of many 'legitimate' industries in the global North – from agriculture in the US, to construction in the Middle East, to catering, cleaning, and childcare almost everywhere. Its centrality to black-market industries (sex, drugs, piracy, and counterfeiting) is at least widely recognized.

Another constant in trafficking and smuggling scenarios is human want and sheer desperation. Young women seeking to escape rural poverty and traditional sex-role constraints; men who lack the resources to play a 'breadwinner' role in their own societies, and eager to believe that opportunity awaits over the horizon – these are the fodder for traffickers and 'agents'. Nowhere is the exploitation more cynical than in the realm of trafficking in young children for coerced labor or rich-country 'adoption'. Such trafficking networks rely on the dire material want of those like 'Kola and his wife Seyi', living in 'a dusty shanty town in Western Nigeria', who 'want to sell their two children – five-year-old Shola and three-year-old Somu – for the price of a modest second-hand car in Britain' – five thousand pounds. So reported David Harrison of the UK *Telegraph*, describing the role of 'agents', both male and female, who exploit the African 'tradition of children moving in with better-off relatives to get a good education'. The agents 'make large sums of money from buying children from desperate families and selling them on within west Africa or, more lucratively, to families in the UK and other Western countries'. For the children exploited in this fashion, the impact is often devastating. In the UK, Harrison writes,

> Trafficked children as young as seven are forced into domestic slavery . . . made to work long hours cooking, cleaning and looking after children, and are deprived of an education. Beatings and sexual abuse are rife. Teenage girls are frequently forced into prostitution. Once they reach 18, psychologically and often physically damaged, they are abandoned with no papers to prove who they are and left vulnerable to further abuse. With nowhere to turn, many fall into crime and the sex trade. Those who go to the authorities for help or are caught committing a crime are likely to be deported. Some are accused of being witches and subjected to exorcism rites. The boy known only as 'Adam', whose torso was found in the Thames in 2001, is believed to have been trafficked to the UK to be used in a 'ritual killing'.

The emerging prohibition regime against human trafficking has placed special emphasis on the sexual exploitation of women and girls. As some of the stories sampled in this section demonstrate, there are solid grounds for recognizing the special vulnerabilities of these groups. But one should also recognize the potential pitfalls of such framings. Women and girls figure prominently in a substantial number of international trafficking and smuggling flows – notably from south-east Asia (Thailand and the Philippines above all) to the Middle East and Europe, and from the Balkans and Central/Eastern Europe to destinations further north and west. They also constitute a majority of those *internally* trafficked in many countries, such as from north-east Thailand to the sex- and entertainment-industry centers in the south, and in China's (increasingly internationalized) market for brides. However, many trafficking and smuggling routes remain traditionally *adult-male* dominated, to the point that undocumented migration serves as a rite of passage for young men in many cultures. This has altered significantly in the past couple of decades, but men still predominate. Their disproportionate victimization in trafficking and smuggling networks is reflected in the gendered death toll of illegal migrants – those sunk on boats attempting to cross from North Africa to Europe, or suffocated in trucks and shipping containers, or dead from thirst in the Arizona desert.

The emphasis on women and children as victims resonates against a cultural backdrop (including a lurid fascination) reminiscent of the campaign against 'White Slavery' in the late nineteenth and early twentieth centuries. The white woman kidnapped by the dark Infidel, and unspeakably defiled at his hands, has its echo in today's discourse of trafficking in women and children – hence the Rome Statute's explicit declaration of 'particular' concern for these groups. This is also a framing around which diverse constituencies can converge – liberal and conservative, religious and secular – greatly boosting the power of the issue to command attention in public and political spheres. It is, however, far from a complete account of human trafficking and smuggling institutions worldwide.

Sexual enslavement

Finally, and relatedly, 'enslavement' has acquired a new dimension under international law, as sexual enslavement – the protracted imprisonment of women for the purpose of rape and sexual exploitation. Intriguingly, it is *only* such enslavement that has prompted prosecutions and led to convictions by international tribunals, as with the Akayesu verdict of 1998. However, 'sexual enslavement' is grouped with rape and other sexual crimes in the Rome Statute, and is explored further in that context (see chapter 7).

5

Arbitrary imprisonment

Uniquely among the crimes against humanity discussed in this book, imprisonment has a legal and 'normal' dimension in all societies. The forcible confinement of individuals accused or convicted of criminal acts is almost universally accepted as among the legitimate coercive powers of the state. Imprisonment itself becomes a crime against humanity when it is arbitrary and/or excessively 'severe' in nature (when rights of due process are abandoned; when imprisonment is accompanied by torture, forced labor, or inhuman conditions producing physical debility or extermination) – and, as always, when it is deployed as part of a systematic or widespread attack on a civilian population.

Imprisonment seems also to have been included as a crime against humanity not *only* because in certain contexts it is criminal in itself, but because by stripping individuals of their rights and confining them, it often sets the stage for the most extreme crimes against humanity: torture, rape, murder, and extermination/genocide. Indeed, in the twentieth century, most of the truly epic campaigns of human destruction were accompanied by arbitrary and systematic imprisonment practices. Instances include not only the Nazis, but also (and especially) communist regimes in the Soviet Union, China, Cambodia, and North Korea.

Democratic states, however, have not been immune to the temptation of using imprisonment strategically, to quell rebellion or 'discipline' civilian populations deemed threatening or suspect. This is especially true in colonial or military occupations, where the democratic norms that prevail at home are suspended abroad, the better to control the 'natives'. A crisis atmosphere domestically can also produce a campaign of arbitrary detention and imprisonment – as during World War II, when the United States and Canada imprisoned tens of thousands of citizens of Japanese descent. I will touch upon imprisonment practices by democratic states later in this chapter. I focus, however, on the far more massively destructive imprisonment practices of twentieth-century totalitarian regimes.

The Nazi camps

The concentration camp was one of the very first institutional manifestations of Nazism. The Dachau prison camp near Munich opened in March 1933, immediately following Hitler's seizure of power. But when the Nazis unleashed the full force of their vision of racial subjugation and extermination, they located their 'death camps' in territories beyond the Reich. German citizens were to be spared the sight of the trains bringing Jews from across Europe to their deaths in the gas chambers; their nostrils would not be assailed by the stink of burning flesh from the crematoria. Instead, the death camps – institutions whose *raison d'être* was the industrial production of corpses: Auschwitz-Birkenau, Treblinka, and a handful of others – were constructed in occupied Poland. Here occurred the infamous 'selections'. For most prisoners – the elderly, all children, all women with children – there was no question of prolonged imprisonment. These people were dispatched directly to the gas chambers.

A small percentage, however, survived. Between the camps on German territory, predominantly for German political prisoners and other national enemies, and the extermination camps, lay the institution of the labor camp (such as the Auschwitz III-Monowitz complex managed by I. G. Farben, where Primo Levi and Elie Wiesel were imprisoned and worked half to death). The labor camps grew in importance as the war turned against the Nazis and manpower shortages grew desperate: overall, between 8 and 12 million people were swept into the Nazi slave-labor system.

The system was especially mortal for ethnic enemies. For Jews above all, work was not a means of earning a slavelike subsistence. Rather, it was designed as a stage in the process of racial annihilation. It wrung a measure of labor value from a prisoner before his or her transfer to the death factory. As Daniel Goldhagen writes in his controversial study of the Holocaust, *Hitler's Willing Executioners*:

> The prevailing German conception of Jewish 'work' [was of] work as temporary exploitation, as a brief detour on the inexorable road to the crematoria or the pits . . . The assumption of extermination and immiseration transformed economic production itself into the handmaiden of the genocidal destruction of the workers.

The result of the single-minded devotion to extermination in the Nazi camp system meant that the only survivors' accounts are those of the relatively privileged: individuals such as Primo Levi, the great chronicler of Auschwitz, who was 'selected' for labor in Auschwitz III. It is sobering to realize, when reading Levi's classic account (see Box opposite), that he was almost unreasonably *lucky*. He was captured and sent to Auschwitz near the end of the war, only a few months before the camp was liberated. He was selected for work; and that work did not kill him before the liberators arrived. Millions of others were not so 'fortunate'.

A PRISONER IN AUSCHWITZ: PRIMO LEVI

Here I am, then, on the bottom. One learns quickly enough to wipe out the past and the future when one is forced to. A fortnight after my arrival I already had the prescribed hunger, that chronic hunger unknown to free men, which makes one dream at night, and settles in all the limbs of one's body. I have already learnt not to let myself be robbed, and in fact if I find a spoon lying around, a piece of string, a button which I can acquire without danger of punishment, I pocket them and consider them mine by full right. On the back of my feet I already have those numb sores that will not heal. I push wagons, I work with a shovel, I turn rotten in the rain, I shiver in the wind; already my own body is no longer mine: my belly is swollen, my limbs emaciated, my face is thick in the morning, hollow in the evening; some of us have yellow skin, others grey. When we do not meet for a few days we hardly recognize each other.

Primo Levi, *Survival in Auschwitz* (New York: Touchstone, 1996), pp. 36–7.

The Soviet Gulag (and Russia today)

Russia under the czarist regimes of the nineteenth and early twentieth centuries was notorious around the world for imprisoning and internally exiling opponents, agitators, and political dissidents. Classic works of literature such as Fyodor Dostoevsky's *House of the Dead* depict the suffering and privations of political prisoners. Prison culture was also popular culture, as attested by the rich tapestry of songs, slang, and humor.

Oppression only spawned more sustained resistance, and by the outbreak of World War I in 1914, the regime of Czar Nicholas II was crumbling. The political order that replaced czarism, however, put the imprisonment strategies of its predecessor in the shade. While the czars had imprisoned dissidents by the dozens or hundreds, the 'Soviet' regime of V. I. Lenin

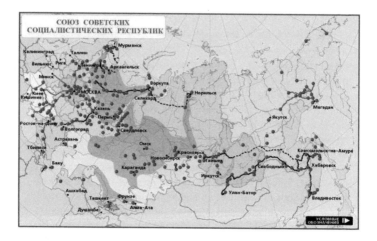

Figure 4 Russian map of the Gulag camp system, showing its extent across the length and breadth of the Soviet Union. The major network in the northeast includes the Kolyma gold fields, where many of the most murderous camps were located. Copyright Memorial, Russia, with the assistance of the Feltrinelli foundation and staff of the Faculty of Geography and Cartography of Moscow State University, http://www.memo.ru

(1917–24) incarcerated them by the tens of thousands. Lenin, in turn, was overshadowed by Joseph Stalin. The agents of 'Stalinism' – the dictatorship established by 1928, which dominated Soviet life until Stalin's death in 1953 – rounded up citizens in their millions, dispatching them to the notorious 'Gulag' system. This was the acronym of the prison camp system Lenin had initiated, which now spread like a virus across the length and breadth of the Soviet Union (see figure 4).

In a protracted fit of power-madness and paranoia, Stalin laid waste to the post-revolutionary generation of Communist Party cadres. In the 'great terror' of 1937–8, over 1.5 million people were arrested, and nearly 700,000 of them shot after interrogation and (often) torture. Hundreds of thousands more were thrown into the vast network of labor camps across the USSR, where they joined millions of others who had run afoul of the system – frequently for something as minor as an off-the-cuff joke, as arbitrary as a family relationship with an accused individual, or as vague as a charge of 'anti-Soviet agitation'. In perhaps the worst irony of all, the Gulag system was bolstered in 1946 by the incarceration of returning Soviet prisoners of war and slave laborers, who were viewed as 'deserters' and 'collaborators' simply for having been captured by the Germans – and having survived to tell the tale.

Those who made it as far as the Gulag camps encountered rampant official violence, malnutrition, crushing overwork, and disease. The death toll was worst in the Arctic and Siberian camps, some of which 'can only be described as extermination centres', according to genocide scholar Leo Kuper. He cites in particular the Kolyma camps,

> where outside work for prisoners was compulsory until the temperature reached -50°C and the death rate among the miners in the goldfields was estimated at about 30 percent per annum; Norilsk, the centre of a group of camps more deadly than Kolyma; and Vorkuta, with temperatures below zero Centigrade for two-thirds of the year and especially deadly for prisoners from southern Russia, who quickly succumbed to the extravagant cold, the exhaustion of hard labor and the starvation diet.

Perhaps a million prisoners died in the Kolyma camps alone – marking the point at which arbitrary imprisonment spills over into mass murder and genocide.

Throughout, it was consistently the case that political prisoners were treated far worse than ordinary criminals. While the latter were deemed capable of reform, the 'politicals' were the scum of the earth – not just lawbreakers, but traitors as well. The

WINTER IN KOLYMA: JANUSZ BARDACH

New dangers presented themselves in the cold. We were only released from work when the temperatures dropped below minus 50 degrees Fahrenheit, and the wind chill was never taken into account. Breathing became painful when the temperature plummeted to minus 25 or minus 30, piercingly so as it approached minus 40 or minus 50. It was dangerous to stop moving . . . Touching a metal tool with a bare hand could tear off the skin, and going to the bathroom was extremely dangerous. A bout of diarrhea could land you in the snow forever . . . Every phase of mining became more difficult in the cold, but the norms, working hours, and food rations remained the same. The lucky ones were able to retain the first category [for the most productive workers], but those who slipped into the second or third food categories began to starve and weaken daily. A difference of only three hundred grams of bread and an additional bowl of soup or oatmeal could mean the difference between life and death . . .

Janusz Bardach and Kathleen Gleeson, *Man is Wolf to Man: Surviving the Gulag* (Berkeley, CA: University of California Press, 1999), pp. 233–4.

urkas, or common criminals, were in fact one of the main means by which political prisoners were terrorized and cowed by the system, as most memoirs of the time attest.

In terms of absolute numbers of prisoners, the Gulag system peaked in the post-World War II era. As part of the 'destalinization' process following the dictator's death, it was rapidly downscaled, and most remaining (political) prisoners were released. Ever since, 'gulag' has served as a generic term for an extensive prison network where the rule of law is absent. It has become a byword for the arbitrary imprisonment practices of dictatorial states – and democratic ones, when activists seek to tar them with the brush of totalitarian practice.

Even after the dismantling of the Gulag, the Soviet prison system remained one of the most brutal in the world. The trend continues in the post-communist period. Russia's may be the world's most murderous prison system: According to François Bonnet, 'every year almost 10,000 prisoners die as a result of malnutrition, overcrowded conditions, or diseases contracted in prison, especially tuberculosis.' The country additionally incarcerates a higher proportion of its population than any other country (though only slightly more than the US – see below).

North Korea

The inheritor of the mantle of totalitarian imprisonment practices, including the widespread use of slave labor, is the ultra-isolated nation of North Korea. Colonized by Japan in the nineteenth century, and divided after World War II into northern and southern zones under different occupation regimes, Korea solidified into two opposed states. Conflict between them flared into open war – with Soviet, Chinese, and US backing – from 1950 to 1953. After a truce was agreed, North Korea under its Stalinist dictator, Kim Il Sung, became 'the Hermit kingdom' – the most tightly sealed and secretive dictatorship in the world.

The fall of communism elsewhere changed nothing in North Korea. The Kim dynasty continued with the ascent of Kim Jong Il following his father's death in 1994. Privation and mass suffering continued to be rampant. What kept North Korea in the headlines, though, was not its atrocious human rights record and widespread famine, but its nuclear brinksmanship. The regime developed and tested a low-yield nuclear weapon, and bartered the resulting fears of destabilization of the volatile Korean peninsula for Western aid and security guarantees.

A constant in this equation was North Korea's version of the gulag. The system of hundreds of detention facilities and

NORTH KOREA: 'WE DID NOT HAVE A TRIAL'

I was only nine years old when my whole family was taken to a concentration camp at night without any charge. The security agents came round to our house and made us pack our things before forcing my father, grandmother, uncle and younger sister into a car to be driven away at dawn. My mother did not come with us because she went through a forced divorce. At that time, I did not fully understand the sorrow of my parents' tears and grief. We did not have a trial. It was not possible to know what crime we had committed. The only thing we knew at that time was that my grandfather had been missing for a few days and that he had been called a traitor to the people. Sometimes my friends would disappear along with their families. The rumours always labelled their families as spies or traitors. When I was young, I believed these as the truth. Almost all North Koreans have knowledge of neighbors who simply disappeared at night. Everybody knows that they had better not ask any questions about their whereabouts. In fact, everyone knows that they were taken to a concentration camp.

Kang Cheol-Hwan, former inmate of Yodeok Political Prison Camp; quoted in Christian Solidarity Worldwide, *North Korea: A Case to Answer, A Call to Act* (New Malden, Surrey: Christian Solidarity Worldwide, 2007), p. 47.

forced-labor camps, combined with pervasive executions, kept a subjugated and starving population in line – or fleeing in desperation across the northern border to China. As under Stalin and Mao, especially pernicious treatment was reserved for political prisoners, who were housed in a network of 'special control institutions' (*Kwanliso*), up to twenty miles in length and half as many wide. Prisoners were summarily shot, tortured, and forced into dangerous slave labor, including 'cleaning the chimneys of Japanese-era munition plants, where there was a high risk of dying from inhaling toxic gases'. According to Young Howard, a South Korean activist working with the US National Endowment for Democracy:

> Prisoners are provided just enough food to be kept perpetually on the verge of starvation. They are compelled by their hunger to eat, if they can get away with it, the food of the labor-camp farm animals, as well as plants, grasses, bark, rats, snakes and anything remotely edible. In committing such desperate acts driven by acute hunger the prisoners simultaneously incur the extreme risk of being detected by an angry security guard and subjected to a brutal, on-the-spot execution. Not surprisingly, the prisoners are quickly reduced to walking skeletons after their arrival. All gulag survivors said they were struck by the shortness, skinniness, premature aging, hunchbacks, and physical deformities of so many of the inmates they saw upon arriving at the gulag. These descriptions parallel those provided by survivors of the Holocaust in infamous camps like Auschwitz.

One of the nongovernmental organizations that has worked to publicize and denounce crimes against humanity in the North Korean prison system is Christian Solidarity Worldwide (see Box opposite). In its report, *North Korea: A Case to Answer, A Call to Act*, issued in 2007, CSW suggested that the conditions inflicted on prisoners had killed hundreds of thousands of inmates over the decades – estimates ranged from 380,000 to over one million. This could qualify as both genocide and the crime against humanity labeled 'extermination':

> The political prison camp policy appears *calculated to cause the death of a large number of persons* who form a part of the population, namely those labelled as 'enemies' who suffer on account of their genuine or alleged political beliefs or other crimes . . . The fact that prisoners are generally seen as 'political enemies', many of whom have no prospect of being released, and that

they are said to be treated inhumanely throughout their imprisonment, indicates a complete disregard for their life.

The Genocide Convention, as we saw in chapter 2, excluded political collectivities as protected groups. The imposition of a systematic and widespread policy calculated to cause massive death and suffering, however, fits well under the rubric of crimes against humanity, which places no limits on the targeted group, beyond its civilian character.

Imprisonment under democracy

Most analyses of mass imprisonment have focused on the major communist and fascist regimes of the twentieth century. And as noted, imprisonment only enters into the framework of crimes against humanity – under international law, at least – when it is deployed arbitrarily, 'in violation of international fair trial guarantees, [and] in the context of a widespread or systematic attack on a civilian population'. A wide latitude exists for states to impose imprisonment policies as they see fit.

Nonetheless, conditions in many 'normal' prison systems may be so inhumane as to constitute a widespread human rights abuse – even a crime against humanity. A lengthy 2005 feature by Michael Wines in *The New York Times*, for example, described 'The Forgotten of Africa, Rotting Without Trial in Vile Jails':

> The inhumanity of African prisons is a shame that hides in plain sight. Black Beach Prison in Equatorial Guinea is notorious for torture. Food is so scarce in Zambia's jails that gangs wield it as an instrument of power. Congo's prisons have housed children as young as 8. Kenyan prisoners perish from easily curable diseases like gastroenteritis . . . Two-thirds of Uganda's 18,000

prison inmates have not been tried. The same is true of three-fourths of Mozambique's prisoners, and four-fifths of Cameroon's. Even in South Africa, Africa's most advanced nation, inmates in Johannesburg Prison have waited seven years to see a judge.

Many of these states are at least ostensibly democratic, with some (Uganda, Kenya, South Africa) regularly cited as models of African governance.

Developed democratic states, too, have been guilty of unjust and arbitrary imprisonment policies as part of a systematic attack on civilian populations. Such practices are more easily carried out abroad than at home – in colonial or neocolonial settings. Caroline Elkins's recent study of the system of concentration camps established in British-ruled Kenya in the 1950s, to combat the 'Mau Mau' uprising among the Kikuyu people, alleges that the camp's ravages meet the UN Convention definition of genocide. Huge numbers were also imprisoned by French forces in colonial Algeria (see chapter 6). Democratic Israel's mass round-up and incarceration of Palestinian men, often with little or no legal recourse available and for terms extending to years, has been a common practice in the Occupied Territories since 1967, and fuel for successive Palestinian uprisings.

A different but equally notable case is that of the United States. The American use of arbitrary detention and forcible imprisonment in the 'war on terror' has attracted widespread condemnation in recent years. It includes the forced disappearance (chapter 8) of suspects 'rendered' to third countries with appalling prison conditions, including the systematic use of torture. There is another dark side to US imprisonment practices, however. With two million of its citizens behind bars, the country has consistently vied with Russia for the title of the world's leading jailer. Ethnic minorities – particularly African-American and Latino men – are disproportionately targeted.

Among the most persistent critics of US prison policy are the world's two leading human rights NGOs, Human Rights Watch and Amnesty International. Of the two, it is Amnesty which has as its founding *raison d'être* the specific issue of prisoners' rights. Amnesty's rise to global prominence, furthermore, attests to the vital role of nongovernmental actors in constructing and monitoring prohibition regimes against crimes against humanity and other human rights abuses.

Amnesty International and the campaign for prisoners' rights

With the exception of the Red Cross, Amnesty International (AI) is probably the best known of all nongovernmental organizations. Its spark – the one that would ignite the candle-behind-barbed-wire in its instantly recognizable logo (designed by Diana Redhouse) – was the Portuguese military dictatorship's detention and imprisonment of a pair of student activists. Peter Benenson, a youngish London lawyer, responded by placing an article in the liberal *Observer* newspaper, denouncing the detentions and pointing to a number of other 'forgotten prisoners' worldwide. The article attracted wide attention and was reprinted internationally. Benenson followed up by planning a network of like-minded activists, persuading publicly prominent figures to sign up with the cause.

Thus, in 1961, was Amnesty International born. It quickly settled on two core norms and a key strategy. The norms: Amnesty would lobby only on behalf of political detainees who had not practised or advocated violence. This was occasionally stretched to permit, for example, AI support for the jailed black South African leader, Nelson Mandela, whose African National Congress (ANC) had adopted a campaign of armed resistance (see chapter 9). Amnesty also enshrined in its statutes an obligation to divide its efforts among the world's principal regions, and among all major political systems. Accordingly, the 'first three adopted prisoners were a Soviet poet, a Jehovah's Witness in Spain, and a communist writer in South Africa'. This did not stop US commentators from denouncing Amnesty as a communist stooge, or Soviet officials decrying it as a capitalist lackey.

The core strategy that Amnesty developed was based on its decentralized network of local committees. Members 'adopted' individual prisoners, and devoted much of their volunteer time and effort to writing letters and 'urgent action' telegrams, addressed to heads of state and other government officials. Such campaigns served a number of purposes. They forged a personal bond between activists and detainees who were separated by thousands of miles. Cumulatively, their impact could be destiny-altering for the 'forgotten prisoner' on the receiving end (see Box below).

'THEN THE NEXT TWO HUNDRED LETTERS CAME . . .': JULIO DE PEÑA VALDEZ

When the two hundred letters came the guards gave me back my clothes. Then the next two hundred letters came and the prison director came to see me. When the next pile of letters arrived, the director got in touch with his superior. The letters kept coming and coming: three thousand of them. The President was informed. The letters still kept arriving and the President called the prison and told them to let me go.

After I was released the President called me to his office for a man-to-man talk. He said: 'How is it that a trade union leader like you has so many friends all over the world?' He showed me an enormous box full of letters he had received and, when we parted, he gave them to me. I still have them.

> Julio de Peña Valdez, a trade-union leader detained in the
> Dominican Republic in 1975; quoted in Jonathan Power,
> *Like Water on Stone: The Story of Amnesty International*
> (London: Penguin, 2001), p. 134.

Even when Amnesty did not succeed in freeing him or her, it could improve conditions of detention and lessen the prisoner's vulnerability to torture, 'disappearance', and summary execution. Amnesty's famous candle-flame was in fact a torchlight, shining into some of the world's most obscure dungeons.

Amnesty grew to be a vital and highly respected information source, producing a body of human–rights reportage that serves as an indispensable record of the abuses and atrocities of the past few decades. Some of these reports derived from 'missions' the organization launched to countries where abuses were alleged to have occurred. Its mission to Argentina in 1976 was essential in constraining the mass detentions and 'disappearances' under the military junta (see also chapter 8); the organization was awarded the Nobel Peace Prize the following year. Several of Amnesty's reports – such as *Torture in the Eighties* (1984) and *Guatemala: The Human Rights Record* (1987) – have become classics, inspiring human rights activism and investigation ever since.

In its durability and the high degree of respect it commands globally, Amnesty has served throughout as a model for 'norm entrepreneurs' who seek to confront and suppress crimes against humanity. Its most notable imitator is Human Rights Watch, which developed out of the Europe-centered Helsinki Watch, with a charter and thematic reach that was broader than Amnesty's. To better compete in the human–rights 'market', Amnesty, too, has expanded beyond its original purview, launching campaigns to defend the rights of women, children, and ethnic minorities. It has also devoted extended attention to prison conditions and abuses in democratic societies, including developed ones such as the UK and US.

The shift has prompted some activists to wonder whether Amnesty risks losing its soul and focus through increasing diversification of its efforts. Others, though, applaud the move beyond the organization's original mandate, arguing that it has successfully 'grafted' Amnesty's credibility and resources onto related and equally worthy issues, allowing for a wider range of rights abuses to be confronted at the state level.

6
Torture

On 1 March 1757 Damiens the regicide [killer of royalty] was condemned 'to make the amende honorable [plea for forgiveness] before the main door of the Church of Paris', where he was to be 'taken and conveyed in a cart, wearing nothing but a shirt, holding a torch of burning wax weighing two pounds'; then, 'in the said cart, to the Place de Grève, where, on a scaffold that will be erected there, the flesh will be torn from his breasts, arms, thighs and calves with red-hot pincers, his right hand, holding the knife with which he committed the said parricide, burnt with sulphur, and, on those places where the flesh will be torn away, poured molten lead, boiling oil, burning resin, wax and sulphur melted together and then his body drawn and quartered by four horses and his limbs and body consumed by fire, reduced to ashes and his ashes thrown to the winds.'

So, indelibly, the philosopher Michel Foucault begins his classic book, *Discipline and Punish*. Foucault's subject is the evolution in thinking and practice of various forms of punishment, from torture to imprisonment to capital punishment. The purpose of his opening pages, nauseating and morbidly fascinating as they are, is to demonstrate through the cruel treatment of Damiens how deeply entrenched were the most barbaric forms of torture in European society at the time.

In the above account, torture is part-and-parcel of the execution ritual. Its more usual function through history has been as a tool of interrogation: a means to elicit information, real or fabricated, from a helpless detainee. It has also regularly been deployed as a strategy of terror and social control – as with its use to enforce religious dogma. Under Catholic regimes, torture became enshrined as an institution of the Holy Inquisition; under Protestantism, it was used on a large scale to extract confessions of supposed witchcraft and complicity with the devil. Adherents of both faiths supported nascent state structures that routinely used torture to enforce political compliance and to discipline subaltern populations.

The word 'torture' derives from the Latin *tortura*, 'twisting', and for good reason. Twisting is standard in many torture practices; an attempted twisting away from the torment is the victim's typical response. The reader may experience something similarly visceral when encountering torture only vicariously, as through this description of a common torture technique, *falanga*, beating of the feet: 'Each blow of the rod is felt not just on the soles of the feet, painfully flexed upward as the club smashes the delicate nerves between the heel and the balls of the foot; the pain shoots up the stretched muscles of the leg and explodes in the back of the skull. The whole body is in agony and the victim writhes like a worm.'

The story of the campaign against torture in the West from the early modern period through the nineteenth century is one of the most inspiring tales on record of mobilization for morally progressive ends. Torture was a defining issue of the Age of Enlightenment. Establishing the rule of Reason meant establishing the rule of Law – with Law defined in a non-tyrannical, non-arbitrary manner. The infliction of severe pain to extract confessions came to be viewed with revulsion by intellectuals such as Voltaire and John Locke. In her book *Tortured Subjects: Pain, Truth, and the Body in Early Modern France*, Lisa Silverman credits the *philosophes* (the French Enlightenment intellectuals) with having redefined the experience of human pain from a divinely inspired, religiously transcendent phenomenon to 'an assault on the rights of individuals' and 'an animalistic experience that threatened the very existence of human society'.

Subaltern populations also increasingly rebelled against the strictures of the authoritarian state, including torture and other forms of cruel and unusual punishment (such as imprisonment for theft of basic foodstuffs, impressment of convicts into military service, and exile to distant colonies). The result was that in the eighteenth and nineteenth centuries, the 'statutory abolition of torture in criminal law swept virtually all of Europe . . . to the extent that Victor Hugo could announce in 1874 that "torture has ceased to exist"'. (Like so many other practices banned at home, however, torture remained alive and well in the European colonies – as depicted in Franz Kafka's short story, 'The Penal Colony'.)

However, the confinement of torture to the margins of Western domestic practice lasted only a few decades. Its resurgence, and its application on a probably unprecedented scale, had much to do with the emergence of modern practices of police repression, particularly against working-class agitators and political dissidents. But it was more inextricably linked with the two great 'totalitarian' ideologies of the twentieth century: fascism and communism.

Torture and totalitarianism

The totalitarian systems of Nazi Germany and the Soviet Union were overwhelmingly *statist*, recognizing no limits on the state's power. Judiciaries were totally subordinated to the executive. Each regime, moreover, viewed itself as besieged by enemies – those of the international Jewish–Bolshevik conspiracy for the Nazis, and those of the international capitalist order for the Soviets. Both the Nazis and Soviets enthusiastically proclaimed the necessity and utility of state terror to confront enemies at home and abroad. Thus, the use of torture became generalized

Figure 5 Karl Schwesig, who was imprisoned by the Nazis in the 1930s, produced this drawing of a Gestapo torture chamber. (Courtesy Gallerie Remmert und Barth, Düsseldorf.)

– throughout the life of the Nazi regime, and for many years in the USSR (though there is evidence that the Stalinist reliance on torture declined over time). Torture was a standard feature of the prison and camp systems instituted in Germany and the USSR – as is examined further in chapters 5 and 8.

Both within and beyond the totalitarian world, torture in the first half of the twentieth century underwent a revolution that led to its transformation into an increasingly sophisticated and scientific practice. This was especially notable with regard to the use of electrical devices, industrial tools, and pharmacological substances. Attendant upon this new sophistication was the increased *professionalization* of torture – including its extension to

'TRUST IN THE WORLD BREAKS DOWN': JEAN AMÉRY

I don't know if the person who is beaten by the police loses human dignity. Yet I am certain that with the very first blow that descends on him he loses something we will perhaps temporarily call 'trust in the world'. Trust in the world includes all sorts of things: the irrational and logically unjustifiable belief in absolute causality perhaps, or the likewise blind belief in the validity of the inductive inference. But more important as an element of trust in the world, and in our context what is solely relevant, is the certainty that by reason of written or unwritten social contracts the other person will spare me – more precisely stated, that he will respect my physical, and with it also my metaphysical, being. The boundaries of my body are also the boundaries of my self. My skin surface shields me against the external world. If I am to have trust, I must feel on it only what I *want* to feel.

At the first blow, however, this trust in the world breaks down . . . With the first blow from a policeman's fist, against which there can be no defense and which no helping hand will ward off, a part of our life ends and it can never again be revived . . . Only in torture does the transformation of the person into flesh become complete. Frail in the face of violence, yelling out in pain, awaiting no help, capable of no resistance, the tortured person is only a body, and nothing else beside that . . . Whoever has succumbed to torture can no longer feel at home in the world.

Jean Améry, *At the Mind's Limits* (New York: Schocken Books, 1986), pp. 28–9, 33, 40 (like Karl Schwesig [see figure 5], Améry was imprisoned and tortured by the Nazis).

the 'caring' professions. The medical doctors who stood by in Nazi or Argentine torture cells, to ensure that prisoners did not die, were accompanied by psychological experts who developed increasingly refined and invisible methods of torture, in part to avoid offending public sensitivities.

Torture and democracy (1): the French in Algeria

Those who wish to control, and cannot do so by suasion, often resort to force. Ordinarily, such recourse is evidence of a critical lack of legitimacy – and the quandary may be particularly acute for colonial governments seeking to discipline restive or rebellious subjects. Since its annexation of the North African territory of Algeria in 1834, France had prided itself on an 'enlightened' colonialism. Algeria was actually accorded the special status of an administrative department of the French republic, giving all Algerians, in theory, access to French citizenship.

In reality, French colonialism, in Algeria as elsewhere (Central Africa, Indochina), was no less exploitative and

---

'I HAD LOST MOST OF MY EMOTIONS': RICHARD JUMA OKETCH

Physically, you portray a mask of who you are, while mentally you are like a furnace . . . [I am still] living the realities of those endless nights. Relentless nightmares, sleeplessness due to fear, anxiety attacks, distrust of people including family members, anti-social behavior, reclusiveness, difficult and hardened personality traits and mood swings, were the invincible [invisible?] scars I lived with. My life remained a total mystery since I allowed no one to penetrate my psyche. I was at most robotic and became workaholic and a perpetual student, as I would fill my time and reduce flashbacks. I made sure I stayed awake past 2:00 a.m. to reduce the hours of the night for fear of persistent nightmares. I had lost most of my sensible emotions . . . I was tired and getting serious injuries as a result of the nightmares. I had lost my interest in living.

Oketch, a prisoner and torture victim under the Idi Amin dictatorship in Uganda, cited in John Conroy, *Unspeakable Acts, Ordinary People: The Dynamics of Torture* (New York: Alfred A. Knopf, 2000), p. 181.

destructive than other colonial forms. It was equally vulnerable to the anticolonial, pro-independence movements that swept the countries of the future 'Third World' from the 1920s on. France's humiliating defeat by Nazi Germany in 1940, and its subordination to Japanese imperial authority in wartime Indochina, further demonstrated the vulnerability of the colonial order. In the decade after the war, the reconstituted French regime found itself confronting violent uprisings on several fronts. In French Indochina, after a failed counterinsurgency effort, the French bowed out of Vietnam, Cambodia, and Laos in 1954.

Algeria was different. Not only was it officially part of France, but there were a million or more *pieds noirs* ('black feet') – white French citizens descended from earlier generations of settlers, or more recent immigrants from the metropole. In fighting the 'Battle of Algiers' (1956–7), French paratroopers found themselves confronting a tenacious enemy occupying the dizzying warren of the *casbah* (old city) in Algiers, the largest city. To break down the network of supporters of the National Liberation Front (FLN), the 'paras' resorted to mass arrest, detention, and systematic torture. 'The most favoured method . . . was the *gégène*, an army signals magneto from which electrodes could be fastened to various parts of the human body – notably the penis.' By one tenable estimate, 'between thirty and forty percent of the entire male population of the Casbah were arrested at some point or other during the course of the Battle of Algiers . . . Disposal of the "inconvenient", of those who died under torture, or who refused adamantly to talk, apparently became prevalent enough to gain the slang expression "work in the woods"'. 'They used to ask for volunteers to finish off the guys who had been tortured', one soldier recalled. As would later occur in the torture states of South America (chapter 8), victims were sometimes flown out to sea in helicopters and dumped there, dead or still living.

Revelations of systematic torture caused an uproar in intellectual circles in France – though like Americans in the 'war on terror' (see below), most remained passively accepting of the torture regime, 'car[ing] for nothing but their outings, their theatres, their vacations . . .'. The protests contributed to the decisive erosion of French authority in Algeria, which finally collapsed and gave way to Algerian independence in 1962. However, on a tactical and even strategic level, torture had succeeded. Resistance in the *casbah* was quelled. The events were later the subject of Gillo Pontecorvo's stupendous film, *The Battle of Algiers* (1966), which graphically depicted the torture of suspects and the wider struggle for control of the *casbah*. It came as no surprise to learn, half a century after the events, that Pontecorvo's film was required viewing in certain US military circles – themselves confronting a tenacious insurgency in Iraq.

The movement against torture and the UN Convention

As we have seen, the post-World War II era witnessed a surge of human-rights and humanitarian activism that arguably matched the flowering of liberalism and Enlightenment thought in the seventeenth and eighteenth centuries. Successive rights instruments – the Universal Declaration of Human Rights (1948), the Geneva Conventions (1949), the Helsinki Final Agreement (1975) – rejected 'torture . . . [and] cruel, inhuman, or degrading treatment or punishment' (in the language of the Universal Declaration).

At the same time, considering the close linkage between torture, arbitrary imprisonment (chapter 5), and forced disappearance (chapter 8), organizations that protested other authoritarian practices often denounced torture as well. The cause was taken up by those speaking on behalf of the detained

THE UN CONVENTION AGAINST TORTURE (10 DECEMBER 1984)

ARTICLE 1

1. For the purposes of this Convention, torture means any act by which severe pain or suffering, whether physical or mental, is intentionally inflicted on a person for such purposes as obtaining from him or a third person information or a confession, punishing him for an act he or a third person has committed or is suspected of having committed, or intimidating or coercing him or a third person, or for any reason based on discrimination of any kind, when such pain or suffering is inflicted by or at the instigation of or with the consent or acquiescence of a public official or other person acting in an official capacity. It does not include pain or suffering arising only from, inherent in or incidental to lawful sanctions [. . .]

ARTICLE 2

1. Each State Party shall take effective legislative, administrative, judicial or other measures to prevent acts of torture in any territory under its jurisdiction.
2. No exceptional circumstances whatsoever, whether a state of war or a threat or war, internal political instability or any other public emergency, may be invoked as a justification of torture.
3. An order from a superior officer or a public authority may not be invoked as a justification of torture.

ARTICLE 3

1. No State Party shall expel, return ('refouler') or extradite a person to another State where there are substantial grounds for believing that he would be in danger of being subjected to torture.
2. For the purpose of determining whether there are such grounds, the competent authorities shall take into account all relevant considerations including, where applicable, the existence in the State concerned of a consistent pattern of gross, flagrant or mass violations of human rights.

and 'disappeared' in Latin America, including the Mothers of the Plaza de Mayo in Argentina (chapter 8) and religious figures around the hemisphere. And the world's leading NGO in the domain of prisoners' rights, Amnesty International – profiled in the preceding chapter – became probably the most vigorous global campaigner against torture.

The consciousness-raising efforts of Amnesty and others contributed to the drafting and (in December 1984) the passing of the UN Convention against Torture and Other Cruel, Inhuman or Degrading Treatment or Punishment (see Box opposite). The Convention was based on the conviction that torture constitutes a fundamental violation of the 'inherent dignity and . . . equal and inalienable rights of all members of the human family', and of 'freedom, justice and peace in the world'. Amnesty went on to publish *Torture in the Eighties*, a seminal work of human-rights reportage.

A critical element in establishing a stable anti-torture regime in at least some parts of the world was the growing emphasis on regional treaty making and institution building. This was especially prominent in Europe and the Americas, where the regional frameworks of the European Union (EU) and the Organization of American States (OAS) allowed for the entrenching of anti-torture legislation and enforcement mechanisms with real 'teeth' (the European Court of Human Rights and the Inter-American Court of American Rights). Elsewhere in the formally 'democratic' world, however, a climate of national emergency was eroding important foundations of the anti-torture regime.

Torture and democracy (2): the US 'war on terror'

In the wake of the 9/11 attacks on the United States, the Bush Administration declared the need for a 'New Paradigm' to confront the terrorist threat. It would be necessary, Vice-President Dick Cheney stated on *Meet the Press*, to:

work through, sort of, the dark side . . . A lot of what needs to be done here will have to be done quietly, without any discussion, using sources and methods that are available to our intelligence agencies . . . It's going to be vital for us to use any means at our disposal, basically, to achieve our objective.

Of all the scandals to result from this edict, the most notorious surrounded revelations from the Abu Ghraib prison near Baghdad. In images transmitted around the world, and in testimony given to an Army investigative commission, abuses were unveiled that included:

Breaking chemical lights and pouring the phosphoric liquid on detainees; threatening detainees with a charged 9mm pistol; pouring cold water on naked detainees; beating detainees with a broom handle and a chair; threatening male detainees with rape . . . sodomizing a detainee with a chemical light and perhaps a broom stick; [and] using military working dogs to frighten and intimidate detainees with threats of attack, and in one instance actually biting a detainee.

An unknown number of detainees were murdered outright or tortured to death, according to 'a military consultant with close ties to the Special Operations community' interviewed by journalist Seymour Hersh. 'What do you call it when people are tortured and going to die and the soldiers know it, but do not treat their injuries? Execution.'

Controversy also swirled over the practice of 'waterboarding', which (in the CIA's own description) involves a prisoner being 'bound to an inclined board, feet raised and head slightly below the feet. Cellophane is wrapped over the prisoner's face and water is poured over him. Unavoidably, the gag reflex kicks in and a terrifying fear of drowning leads to almost instant pleas to bring the treatment to a halt'. CIA officers who tested the treatment on themselves 'lasted an average of 14 seconds before caving in'.

What was most striking about these crimes was the direct involvement of US personnel. The tendency in the post-World War II era has been for great powers to 'outsource' atrocities to Third World clients. Now, as Naomi Klein points out, atrocity was being 'insourced', directly supervised by the US government. In Iraq, by late 2005, the campaign of torture and murder waged by Shi'ite death squads run from the Interior Ministry had approached levels comparable to or even exceeding those of the despotic Saddam Hussein regime. As in Latin America in the 1970s and 1980s, this was 'a savage war in the shadows', in which victims, mostly Sunni Muslims, 'are arrested and disappear for months. Bodies appear every week of men, and sometimes women, executed with their hands tied behind their backs. Some have been grotesquely mutilated with knives and electric drills before their deaths.'

The resurgence of torture in post-Hussein Iraq was buttressed by a Bush Administration policy that constituted 'a comprehensive assault on our traditional understanding of the whole legal regime relating to torture', according to Columbia Law School professor Jeremy Waldron. The strategy was to define 'torture' in a way that excluded, and thus permitted, the application of measures that appeared to fall within the boundaries of the Torture Convention definition. Typical was the August 2002 declaration by Assistant Attorney General Jay S. Bybee that the term 'torture' 'covers only extreme acts . . . Where the pain is physical, it must be of an intensity akin to that which accompanies serious physical injury such as death or organ failure.' Even where such torture *was* used, those inflicting it could still be exculpated: 'necessity or self-defense could provide justifications that would eliminate any criminal liability . . . '

There was always the possibility, however, that a dissident US judge or suddenly galvanized Congress could disrupt the

A 'LAWLESS TORTURE POLICY': LETTERS TO *THE NEW YORK TIMES*

To the Editor:

[The revelations about US use of torture in interrogations] make me feel sick and desperate about what this president has done, and continues to do, to our once-proud country in only seven years. Could he have done more to debase us if he had set out purposely to destroy us, our economy, our moral values and our dignity?

Monica Mori, Chicago, Oct. 4, 2007

Since when does trashing civil liberties and rights defend democracy? How did we come to have leaders who exhibit qualities of those from whom they claim to protect us? Is this American democracy?

Kenneth Aaron, Portland, Ore., Oct. 4, 2007

Only by restoring the rule of law can the United States repair the damage done by the Bush administration's lawless torture policy . . . It is time for the law to be enforced, for perpetrators to be held accountable, for Congress to explicitly prohibit the CIA's enhanced methods, and for American institutions and values to be reclaimed.

Leonard S. Rubenstein, Pres., Physicians for Human Rights,
Washington, Oct. 4, 2007
The New York Times, 5 October 2007

smooth functioning of the new understanding. Where possible, then, suspects could be 'rendered' to other countries well known to practice torture, masking the US role and ensuring that no meaningful oversight prevailed. 'Extraordinary rendition' is examined further in the context of forced disappearance, in chapter 8.

Torture and bystanders

While torturers are a relatively small group, widespread torture is impossible unless a critical mass of those in positions of authority play along or turn a blind eye. 'Bystander' behavior extends to the society at large. With the rarest of exceptions, torture is closeted from public view, with only the occasional cry heard through the walls of the detention centre. The rest is rumor and gossip. To further conceal their actions, torturers may resort to techniques that leave marks on the psyche more than on the external physique. It was easy for the 'good German' of yesteryear to ignore the Nazis' systematic use of torture in part because the Gestapo had perfected methods that did not kill or permanently incapacitate the prisoner. In 2007, public apathy was also pronounced in the wake of revelations of the Bush regime's authorization of 'enhanced interrogation' tactics that were remarkably similar to those deployed by the Gestapo. As conservative commentator Andrew Sullivan summarized the parallels:

> Is 'enhanced interrogation' torture? One way to answer this question is to examine history. The phrase has a lineage. *Verschärfte Vernehmung*, enhanced or intensified interrogation, was the exact term innovated by the Gestapo to describe what became known as the 'third degree'. It left no marks. It included hypothermia, stress positions and long-time sleep deprivation. The United States prosecuted it as a war crime in Norway in 1948 . . . The Nazis even argued that 'the acts of torture in no case resulted in death. Most of the injuries inflicted were slight and did not result in permanent disablement.' This argument is almost verbatim that made by John Yoo, the Bush administration's house lawyer . . . The penalty for those [Nazis] who were found guilty was death. This is how far we've come.

Eroding the anti-torture regime

The evolution of the international ban on torture is in central respects a tale of *de*volution – of the erosion and decline of the prohibition regime in question. Widespread revulsion against the use of torture as a judicial tool resulted in its progressive banishment across Europe and around the world in the nineteenth and early twentieth centuries. However, the totalitarian governments of the first half of the twentieth century – and colonial, postcolonial, and neocolonial orders of the postwar era – rediscovered torture as a means of extracting information, terrorizing populations, and suppressing dissidence. Even Western democracies resorted to such measures in times of national crisis, as with the widespread use of torture by Great Britain to suppress Irish Republican Army (IRA) terrorism, and by the US in waging the 'war on terror'.

The trajectory sketched here is a reminder that protections and prohibitions against atrocities can not only wax but wane. Humanity's course is not a linear one of forward progress, but a series of advances (often halting) and retreats (sometimes dramatic). In parts of the world where torture once ran rampant, such as Europe and Latin America, it has been radically curtailed – at least as a generalized tool of state terror. Elsewhere, however, torture either has never gone away, or has re-insinuated itself, incrementally and surreptitiously. Its resurfacing attests to torture's enduring attraction as a mechanism of 'security' and social control. Its apparently spreading appeal, amidst little protest, is a blot on the reputation of the civilized world – and a 'cancer of democracy', as Pierre Vidal-Naquet put it the title of a 1963 book.

The 'cancer' that Vidal-Naquet referred to 'was not the torture itself, but the public indifference to it that eroded and rendered meaningless even the most explicit protections afforded by civil rights and public law'. *All that is necessary for the triumph of evil is that good people do nothing.* This maxim's attribution to the eighteenth-century British intellectual Edmund Burke may be suspect, but the insight is no less apt.

7

Rape and sexual crimes

Rape was defined in the Rome Statute of the International Criminal Court as the 'invas[ion of] the body of a person by conduct resulting in penetration, however slight, of any part of the body of the victim or of the perpetrator with a sexual organ, or of the anal or genital opening of the victim with any object or any other part of the body'. Such an invasion must be accomplished by means of 'force, or by threat of force or coercion', or by exploiting a coercive situation. Rape exists in the Statute alongside other sexual crimes against humanity, including 'sexual slavery, enforced prostitution, forced pregnancy, enforced sterilization, or any other form of sexual violence of comparable gravity'.

In the course of human conflict, such crimes have overwhelmingly, and justifiably, been framed in terms of male violence against women and girls. (I will offer some comments about men and boys as victims toward the end of the chapter.) While rape and sexual crimes against females occur with numbing regularity in 'peacetime', they tend to be pervasive in conflict situations. Traditionally, women have been viewed as a 'spoil' of war and conquest. Sexual violations of their integrity run parallel with, and vividly symbolize, the territorial violation of invasion and occupation. What is distinctive about the last century, and this new one, is (1) the growing systematization of rape as a military and paramilitary *policy*; (2) the increasing use of rape as a tool of terror – a strategy of counterinsurgency, ethnic cleansing, and even genocide; and (3) the efforts by women's groups and international organizations to confront rape, prosecute its perpetrators, and render assistance to its victims.

Mass rape: the twentieth-century experience

The World War II period – including its prelude and immediate aftermath – witnessed some of the most intensive campaigns of mass rape on record. They began with the Japanese 'Rape of Nanjing' in 1937, where the murder of some 200,000 Chinese men was accompanied by the rape-murder of tens of thousands of Chinese women. Even larger in scale were the rapes perpetrated by Soviet troops in occupied Germany. Beginning with the first conquests of German territory in 1944, and continuing long after the German surrender in May 1945, the rape of German women was generalized. Perhaps two million women were assaulted, most of them multiple times, in the closing phase of the most gargantuan military conflict of all time, and in acts of vengeance and drunken exploitation thereafter.

Rape was declared a crime against humanity at Nuremberg, but not prominently. Rather, it was subsumed under the category 'other inhumane acts' in Article 5(c) of the tribunal's Charter. Rape did not figure in the verdicts finally issued – perhaps because Soviet forces had been sullied by their mass rapes of German women, and prosecutors did not wish to allow defense lawyers recourse to a *tu quoque* defense ('we're not guilty because you did it too'). The Tokyo Tribunal, for its part, prosecuted and convicted Japanese officers in command of the forces who unleashed the Rape of Nanjing in 1937–8, and rape was among the crimes enumerated in the indictments. But another Japanese crime – the kidnapping and trafficking of women in occupied countries for the purpose of sexual exploitation –

would require decades to come to light. Only in the 1990s did international attention begin to focus on the 200,000 so-called 'comfort women' – Korean, Filipina, Chinese, Japanese – and their demands for redress.

These twentieth-century mass rapes, despite their huge scale, were broadly in keeping with millennia of war and genocidal practice. However, the next campaign of massive sexual violence, in Bangladesh in 1971, was of a different character. Troops from West Pakistan, seeking to destroy the Bengali national identity that had fueled an independence drive in East Pakistan, raped and forcibly impregnated Bengali women by the tens or hundreds of thousands. At the same time, they killed younger Bengali men in enormous numbers (likely a million or more – see chapter 2). Both gendered strategies aimed to intimidate the Bengali population into quiescence, and terrorize it into mass flight.

After the genocide, the new Bangladeshi government sought to validate women rape victims as 'heroes' of independence, and to encourage their marriage to male independence activists. The program ebbed, though, in the face of traditional stereotypes of the raped woman as sullied and 'dishonored'. Feminist opinion and commentary on rape as an international issue began to stir, as typified by the discussion of the Bangladeshi crimes in Susan Brownmiller's 1975 book, *Against Our Will: Men, Women, and Rape* (see 'Further Reading'). The surge of Western women's activism at this time pushed the issue of rape and sexual violence to a more prominent position on both national and international policy agendas. Feminists worked to reconceptualize rape as an assault on women's rights and integrity, not their 'honor' as constructed by a patriarchal order. They sought to enshrine such an understanding in relevant legal instruments, and to build new institutions of intervention and redress at all levels, from the local to the global. As one result, in many cities of the developing world, women's mobilizations have prompted the introduction of female police officers and counselors to investigate cases of alleged rape and provide aid to survivors – an important advance in persuading victims to come forward and interact with a justice system previously unresponsive to their needs.

With this institutional backdrop in place, the issue of rape was poised to move to the forefront of international public debate. The trigger was the Balkans wars of the 1990s (see chapters 2 and 3). In Bosnia-Herzegovina, Serbian men were generally the perpetrators, though Muslim and Croat soldiers and militia raped also. Rape and forced impregnation were used to terrify and humiliate ethnically defined populations and to 'cleanse' them from territories prized by the perpetrators. The dimension of rape-as-policy seemed pronounced, as Yugoslav journalist Slavenka Drakulic wrote shortly after the first great wave of 'cleansings' in 1992–3:

> What seems to be unprecedented about the rapes of Muslim women in Bosnia (and, to a lesser extent, the Croat women too) is that there is a clear political purpose behind the practice. The rapes in Bosnia are not only a standard tactic of war, they are an organized and systematic attempt to cleanse (to move, resettle, exile) the Muslim population from certain territories Serbs want to conquer in order to establish a Greater Serbia. The eyewitness accounts and reports state that women are raped everywhere and at all times, and victims are of all ages, from 6 to 80. They are also deliberately impregnated in great numbers . . . held captive and released only after abortion becomes impossible. This is so they will 'give birth to little Chetniks [Serb paramilitaries],' the women are told.

Estimates of the total number of females assaulted during the Bosnian conflict, and in other theaters of the Yugoslav wars, range from 10,000 to 50,000. The rape of women was accompanied by the large-scale murder of predominantly Muslim males, most notoriously the execution of up to 8,000 Muslim men and boys at Srebrenica in July 1995. A substantial and systematic degree of rape and sexual violence against men was also evident – notably among the tens of thousands of captives, mostly Bosnian Muslims and Croats, who passed through Serb detention centers and concentration camps (see further below).

In 1994, in order to stage at least a symbolic intervention, the members of the UN Security Council established an International Criminal Tribunal for the Former Yugoslavia

'E.', A 16-YEAR-OLD MUSLIM GIRL, DESCRIBES HER RAPE BY SERB PARAMILITARIES

Several Chetniks arrived. One, a man around 30, ordered me to follow him into the house. I had to go. He started looking for money, jewelry and other valuables. He wanted to know where the men were. I didn't answer. Then he ordered me to undress. I was terribly afraid. I took off my clothes, feeling that I was falling apart. The feeling seemed under my skin; I was dying, my entire being was murdered. I closed my eyes, I couldn't look at him. He hit me. I fell. Then he lay on me. He did it to me. I cried, twisted my body convulsively, bled. I had been a virgin.

He went out and invited two Chetniks to come in. I cried. The two repeated what the first one had done to me. I felt lost. I didn't even know when they left. I don't know how long I stayed there, lying on the floor alone, in a pool of blood.

My mother found me. I couldn't imagine anything worse. I had been raped, destroyed and terribly hurt. But for my mother this was the greatest sorrow of our lives. We both cried and screamed. She dressed me.

I would like to be a mother some day. But how? In my world, men represent terrible violence and pain. I cannot control that feeling.

Cited in Slavenka Drakulic, 'Rape After Rape After Rape',
The New York Times, 13 December 1992

(ICTY) at The Hague in Holland. The visibility of the Bosnian rape issue as an international *cause célèbre* ensured that it would feature prominently on the court's prosecutorial agenda.

Some feminist scholars carried the issue further by alleging that what was taking place in Bosnia was *genocidal* rape. Feminist legal theorist Catharine MacKinnon appears to have made the first reference to 'rape as genocide', but it was Beverly Allen, in her 1996 book *Rape Warfare*, who defined 'genocidal rape' as 'a military policy of rape for the purpose of genocide'. Rape was genocide when it served as a prelude to the murder of a woman or girl on the basis of her national, ethnic, or religious identity. But it was not coterminous with the physical killing of the victim. Rather, rape could also be genocidal by bringing about the 'destruction' of the group through the undermining and dissolution of its bonds of communal solidarity.

Some feminist scholars rejected this emphasis on rape-as-genocide, arguing, among other things, that it risked distracting attention from rape by prioritizing the broader genocidal dimension. But the thesis received grim backing from the apocalyptic events in Rwanda between April and July 1994 (see chapter 2). The rape of Tutsi women – often including sexual mutilation – was epidemic throughout the Rwandan genocide. Tens of thousands of women, at a minimum, were killed immediately following sexual attack. The assaults continued against Tutsi women who were preserved alive, however temporarily, to serve as sex slaves for Hutu *génocidaires*. Many Tutsi women were impregnated by Hutu men. Uncounted thousands, exposed to repeated gang rape by Hutu militia members, were infected by the HIV virus.

This was rape used as a strategy to destroy the Tutsi ethnic group in Rwanda. It was not intended as a terror device to set populations to flight, since Tutsis – including Tutsi women – were not permitted to escape. Like Jewish women at Nazi hands, they were destined for extermination. The difference in the Rwandan case is that no racial taboo prevented their large-scale sexual enslavement and exploitation prior to extermination. Only the military victory of the Rwandan Patriotic Front (RPF) in July 1994 allowed some of these captive Tutsi women to evade death.

The stunning speed and scale of the Rwandan genocide prompted the same 'international community' that had stood by lackadaisically as the killing unfolded to establish another ad hoc criminal tribunal for Rwanda. One of its early and most ground-breaking judgments was the Akayesu verdict of September 1998, when Jean-Paul Akayesu, a Rwandan bourgmeister, was found guilty of supervising acts of rape and sexual enslavement of Tutsi women. According to the tribunal, this sexual violence not only accompanied genocide, but *constituted* it.

SEXUAL ENSLAVEMENT IN RWANDA

I don't remember the date, but it was in the month of April [1994], when we heard that the interahamwe [genocidal Hutu militia] were coming . . . I managed to run away with some others . . . Then the interahamwe took us, and shared us out among themselves. Some were raped, some were killed . . . They separated out the girls and put them on one side and told them, 'You, we are not going to kill you.' . . . The one who took me was from [President] Habyarimana's home in the north-west. His name was Bugimulunje. First, there was another one who chose me. But Bugimulunje wanted me, and he paid a thousand francs to the other man so that he could have me instead. There was another girl called Thérèse, she was taken too, and one other girl. The men had to pay, to give money to those guys who were holding them, to drink. Bugimulunje kept me for one week and a half. I was raped every night.

Testimony of 'Catherine', in African Rights, *Rwanda: Death, Despair, and Defiance*, rev. edn (London: African Rights, 1995), pp. 774–5.

This dimension of sexual enslavement merits brief further exploration. It derives from the broader injunction against slavery (chapter 4), and is specifically referenced as a crime against humanity in the Rome Statute's 'Elements of Crimes'. The Bosnian and Rwandan practices of detention for purposes of rape clearly shaped the specific references to sexual enslavement, which occurs when 'the perpetrator exercise[s] any or all of the powers attaching to the right of ownership over one or more persons, such as by purchasing, selling, lending or bartering such a person or persons, or by imposing on them a similar deprivation of liberty', and when 'the perpetrator caused such person or persons to engage in one or more acts of a sexual nature'.

As the Balkan and Rwandan examples suggest, sexual slavery has predominantly been prosecuted in the context of genocidal campaigns. Empirically, however, there is a substantial spillover between sexual enslavement and human trafficking, especially trafficking in women and girls. Notably, the sexual enslavement provisions of the 'Elements of Crimes' document (Article 7(1)(g)-2) are followed immediately by the 'crime against humanity of enforced prostitution' (Article 7(1)(g)-3), in which, pursuing a 'pecuniary [monetary] or other advantage',

> the perpetrator caused one or more persons to engage in one or more acts of a sexual nature by force, or by threat of force or coercion, such as that caused by fear of violence, duress, detention, psychological oppression or abuse of power, against such person or persons or another person, or by taking advantage of a coercive environment or such person's or persons' incapacity to give genuine consent.

Given the prominence of human trafficking in the international debate, and the increasing adoption by international feminist movements of sexual exploitation as a core mobilizing issue, one might expect to see sexual enslavement deployed in legal cases where (for example) paramilitary groups are accused of trafficking and/or prostituting women to fund their operations. However, because such practices must be part of a 'widespread or systematic attack' on civilians in order to qualify as crimes against humanity, a focus on sexual enslavement as a strategy of genocide and ethnic cleansing will probably remain.

Congo and Darfur

The new millennium was a period of continued international activism around women's rights and the violence done to females the world over. But however ringing the declarations and however notable the advances in international law, they could do little to stem violence against women on the most conflict-riven continent, Africa. The genocide in Darfur, Sudan, which began in 2003 and continues today, has featured the systematic rape and forcible expulsion of women and girls, accompanied by the killing of men. Women and girls who succeeded in reaching refugee camps found themselves liable to assault within those camps, or while ranging long distances for water and firewood. In an indication of the calculus of desperation that prevails in such circumstances, women often rejected men's offers to take their place, knowing that any men who were captured would be murdered rather than 'only' raped.

In eastern Congo, sexual violence against women had reached 'almost unimaginable' levels by late 2007, exhibiting 'an intensity and frequency [that] is worse than anywhere else in the world' (in the assessment of John Holmes, the UN Under-Secretary General for Humanitarian Relief). In 1994, as Tutsi rebel forces overwhelmed the Hutu Power regime in Rwanda, genocidal killers and large numbers of ordinary Hutus flooded into eastern Congo. The ensuing refugee crisis overshadowed (and obscured) the genocide in foreign media and political spheres. More significantly for the longer term, it set off a vicious civil war, and then an international conflict. Congo became 'Africa's World War', drawing in a dozen other countries as fighters and sustainers of the fighters.

The geographic core of the violence remained the lawless lands of eastern Congo (the provinces of North and South Kivu, adjacent to Rwanda). There, militia formed from Hutu *génocidaires* re-established the 1994 pattern of genocidal killing combined with the rape and sexual mutilation of women. Other paramilitary forces roaming the region followed suit. The world's largest UN peacekeeping force – 17,000 strong – was dispatched, but proved nearly powerless to protect civilians. Peacekeepers had grown more attuned to the gendered vulnerabilities of women and girls in wartime, but their attempts to intervene in the epidemic of sexual violence were limited to stationing troop-carriers in the Congolese countryside and leaving their headlights blazing all night. Even this marginal measure of security was enough to draw thousands of villagers to sleep in the glow cast by the lights. Sometimes, reprehensibly, the peacekeepers were part of the problem. In 2004, UN peacekeepers from Morocco, Nepal, South Africa, and elsewhere were accused of crimes ranging from rape to pedophilia and involvement in prostitution. Some 180 peacekeepers had been disciplined by late 2006.

By 2008, war and genocide in Congo had killed at least 4 million people – the largest death toll since World War II. Rape and sexual violence were occurring on a likewise unmatched scale. The rape – frequently gang rape – of women by both Congolese forces and roving Hutu militias had become so insti-tutionalized that it was 'almost a cultural phenomenon', in John Holmes's estimation. All females were in danger. A *New York Times* profile of Congolese gynecologist Denis Mukwege in October 2007 described ten rape victims *a day* arriving at his small clinic. Many had not only been sexually violated, but 'so sadistically attacked from the inside out, butchered by bayonets and assaulted with chunks of wood, that their reproductive and digestive systems are beyond repair'.

Forced pregnancy

> The perpetrator confined one or more women forcibly made pregnant, with the intent of affecting the ethnic composition of any population or carrying out other grave violations of international law . . .
>
> Rome Statute, 'Elements of Crimes'

Patriarchal (male-dominant) societies are overwhelmingly also *patrilineal* societies: descent is traced through the male bloodline. Ethnic groups and nation-states, meanwhile, are 'imagined communities', as the historian Benedict Anderson recognized. They rely upon collective visions of a shared identity. When patriarchy/patrilineality is combined with ethnic nationalism, one has the recipe for the use of forced pregnancy as a tool of genocide and 'ethnic cleansing'.

The male perpetrator believes that in his seed resides the ethnicity of his tribe. Forcibly impregnating a woman of an opposing group, and either confining the victim for the term of her pregnancy or leaving her with the bleak (and perhaps dangerous) choice of bearing an 'alien' child or aborting the fetus, accomplishes a multifaceted assault on the targeted ethnic group. The 'imagined community' of the tribe is increased if the pregnancy is carried to term – with the added incentive, for the perpetrator, that his seed has now germinated in the 'alien' group. Moreover, for the duration of the pregnancy, the targeted female is unavailable for reproduction within her own group. Expression of her sexual being is further impeded by post-assault trauma, and shunning by members of her own community. The masculine roles of out-group men, too, are undermined and eroded by their failure to prevent the invasion and occupation of their lands, property – and loved ones.

For all these reasons, forced pregnancy has been firmly entrenched as a component of sexual crimes against women and crimes against humanity in general. Initiatives such as those launched in Bangladesh after the 1971 genocide, and in Bosnia-Herzegovina in the 1990s, aimed to assist women survivors of these attacks, and respond to their distinctive needs. However, little if any attention was devoted to the *child* that resulted from the forced impregnation. International relations scholar R. Charli Carpenter has worked to counter this 'systematic neglect of children's rights in accounts of rape', arguing that while 'children may be tacitly acknowledged as victims' in prevailing discourse, 'their rights are never articulated directly', and 'their fate is reduced to an interesting issue to ponder rather than as a set of crimes to observe and address'.

In fact, Carpenter contends, the destiny of the children in forced-impregnation strategies is no less central than that of their mothers. If they are isolated and marginalized by their communities, the destructive impact is similar to that upon a female rape survivor. Sometimes states may even deny children citizenship on the basis of their 'alien' parentage. But the perspectives of women rape survivors and the children they bear are sharply different, and Carpenter argues that attention to children 'requires detachment from the discourse of women's violation and engagement with the standpoint of the child vis-à-vis state and international law'.

Forced sterilization

The perpetrator deprived one or more persons of biological reproductive capacity . . . neither justified by the medical or hospital treatment of the person or persons concerned nor carried out with their genuine consent.

Rome Statute, 'Elements of Crimes'

The inclusion of forced sterilization under the rubric of crimes against humanity derives from the revulsion spawned by revelations of Nazi practices during World War II. Entire classes of people – including the mentally and physically handicapped, homosexuals, and Roma (Gypsies) – were destined for mass sterilization. Hundreds of thousands were actually sterilized under laws such as the Law for the Prevention of Offspring with Hereditary Diseases, enacted with indecent speed once the Nazis seized power in 1933. Especially horrific to Western publics after the war were the grotesque 'medical' experiments conducted in concentration camps, including those involving castration, sterilization, and genetic manipulation.

Forced sterilization practices have a much longer heritage, however, especially as a component of *eugenics* – practices aimed at 'improving' the mental, physical, or racial 'stock' of a given society. Eugenics remains closely associated with the Nazi racial ideology of Aryan *Übermensch* (superman) and Jewish-Slavic-Gypsy *Untermensch* (subhuman). But Nazi practice was merely the crest of a wave that had gathered force earlier and elsewhere, notably in the US, Canada, and the UK. Forced sterilization of Native peoples, the handicapped, and convicted criminals was widespread in these countries during the first half of the twentieth century.

Since World War II, accusations of forced sterilization as part of a 'systematic and widespread' assault on civilian populations have occasionally been raised, most notably in the context of Chinese occupation policy in Tibet. They have rarely held up under scrutiny, however. A second tier of acts includes coercive birth-control measures of the kind instituted in India under Indira Gandhi during the 1970s. A case can be made that the luring (and allegedly tricking) of poor Indian men into under-going vasectomies was a systematic assault on the poor and dispossessed. However, just as 'normal' and even abusive impris-onment practices do not necessarily constitute a crime against humanity, so has the international community been reluctant to characterize as crimes the population-control practices of Third World states that sometimes spill over into excessive and abusive practices.

The new attention in the 1990s and 2000s to the phenom-enon of mass rape means that the forced sterilization provisions of crimes–against–humanity legislation are perhaps most likely to be activated in cases where sexual attack leaves women incapable of bearing children. In the Rwandan genocide, for example, Human Rights Watch reports that 'women were gang raped, raped repeatedly with objects, and subjected to outrageous brutality, some of which involved mutilating women's sexual organs. Some of these attacks left women so physically injured that they may never be able to bear children.' If this is not charged as genocide (Article II(d) of the Genocide Convention forbids 'prevent[ing] births within the group'), it may be pros-ecuted as a crime against humanity, related to but distinct from the crime of rape.

Rape and sexual crimes against men and boys

I noted that a key element of rapes of women in war is to humil-iate enemy males – to drive home their failure to protect 'their' daughters, wives, and womenfolk. In highly patriarchal societies, the rape of women likewise obstructs family relationships in the long term by building a wall of shame around women – leading to their unjust, often violent alienation from their menfolk and from the wider community. This is part of the story of sexual violence against women. It is also a form of sexualized violence against males, as has long been recognized in feminist commentary. Another dimension of sexual violence, however, has only recently begun to receive sustained attention. This is the direct infliction of rape and sexual violence on males.

In a groundbreaking study of such atrocities, British legal scholar Sandesh Sivakumaran points to the prevalence of such atrocities in the long history of human conflict. In ancient times, victory was celebrated not only by genocidally exterminating or enslaving the subject population, but by castrating males of the vanquished group en masse. Graphically demonstrating the subjugation of out-group men – and not incidentally inhibiting the reproduction of the group itself – have remained central motivations for such violence. In the Balkans in the 1990s, male prisoners were raped by blunt instruments, forced to rape other male prisoners, and subjected to ruthless genital attack, including castration. Such strategies were joined with sexual assaults against females in campaigns of genocide and 'ethnic cleansing'. Humiliating a male enemy through sexual violence against him suggests 'not only that he is a lesser man, but also that his ethnicity is a lesser ethnicity', unworthy of occupying lands that the perpetrator covets.

Sexual violence against men and boys in the Balkans is one of the tiny handful of such cases to have received a small measure of attention in mass media and from international tribunals. The violence occurred overwhelmingly under conditions of detention and imprisonment. Everywhere in the world, it is in this institutional context that sexual violence against males is most widespread. Rape through penile penetration features prominently, but probably more common is genital attack and rape with an inanimate object such as a truncheon or bottle.

Sivakumaran points to signs that international legal and humanitarian agencies are beginning to awaken to the issue of systematic sexual violence against males in wartime. Detailed investigations and constructive prescriptions are clearly called for. The benefits could extend beyond men, to the women and children in survivors' immediate families, who often bear the brunt of a male survivor's rage and humiliation.

8

Forced disappearance

On 7 December 1941, Japanese planes bombed the US naval base at Pearl Harbor. Nazi Germany, poised to join with its fascist Japanese ally in declaring war on the United States, launched its own assault on 7 December: a sweeping political crackdown in Nazi-occupied Western Europe. The campaign was dubbed *Nacht und Nebel* – 'Night and Fog'. The phrase, used as the title of one of the first postwar documentaries about Nazi crimes, became a symbol of what would soon become known as the Holocaust. In fact, though, Night and Fog targeted generally non-Jewish political dissidents.

Persecuting and killing political opponents was nothing new in Nazi strategy. Communists, socialists, journalists, trade union leaders, and others were among the first victims of the concentration camps in the 1930s. The occupation of Western Poland in 1939 was similarly accompanied by systematic murders of the Polish political class and intelligentsia. What was distinctive about Night and Fog was the strategy of *disappearing* opponents, as a way not only of neutralizing them, but of traumatizing their intimates, and of maintaining the population in a state of terror and uncertainty. As SS Reichsführer Heinrich Himmler instructed the Gestapo, 'an effective and lasting deterrent' of political enemies could 'be achieved only by the death penalty *or by taking measures which will leave the family and the population uncertain as to the fate of the offender*' (emphasis added). Field Marshall Wilhelm Keitel echoed Himmler's comments, stressing the point that 'the relatives of the criminals [should] not know the fate of the criminal'. The prisoner was to be deported to Germany for 'further treatment'. The essence of the 'deterrent' lay in the fact that 'A. The prisoners will vanish without a trace. B. No information may be given as to their whereabouts or their fate.'

The requirement of *habeas corpus* (roughly, 'produce the body') was a cornerstone of emerging conceptions of human and civil rights. Opponents or suspected dissidents could not simply and permanently 'disappear' into a tyrant's jail cells and torture chambers. If detained, they had the right to be released promptly, if not formally charged; and if charged, to receive a fair and public trial. Night and Fog deliberately subverted this foundation of European constitutional and common law. In addition, the method offered a number of bureaucratic conveniences. Protests and petitions, from the church or from international organizations and governments, were harder to deliver when the fate of the 'disappeared' person was unknown or the subject of vague rumor. The public could be kept politically incapacitated by low-level fear, and the passive 'bystander' stance of the majority encouraged by avoidance of provocative acts of public violence.

In an important precedent for the later incorporation of forced disappearance as a crime against humanity, the Nuremberg tribunal specifically referenced Night and Fog as 'inhumane', noting that 'After these civilians arrived in Germany, no word of them was permitted to reach the country from which they came, or their relatives; even in cases when they died awaiting trial the families were not informed, the purpose being to create anxiety in the minds of the family of the arrested person.'

By instituting Night and Fog, the Nazis built on repressive practices implemented in diverse dictatorial settings (including colonial ones) during the first decades of the twentieth century.

A classic case is that of Joseph Stalin (see chapter 5). During the urban political terror that Stalin launched in the late 1920s and 1930s, entire populations were paralyzed by fear of a knock on their door in the middle of the night, leading to them being taken away by the secret police and 'disappearing', either for rapid execution in a dungeon or for protracted incarceration in the Gulag camp system (see chapter 6). 'Most of us didn't live in any real sense,' wrote a survivor of the period, Nadezhda Mandelstam, 'but existed from day to day, waiting anxiously for something until the time came to die . . . In the years of the terror, there was not a home in the country where people did not sit trembling at night, their ears straining to catch the murmur of passing cars or the sound of the elevator.'

Stalinism remained a byword of police terror until the dictator's death in 1953. Even thereafter, the vast size of the Soviet Union, the extent of its empire in Eastern Europe, and the secretiveness of the state-socialist bureaucracy ensured that an element of 'disappearance' remained in the ordinary workings of the system. Forced exile, a millennia-old strategy, was also common, and represented a 'disappearance' in its own right – eliminating the capacity to shape events through political participation. And just when it seemed that the Soviet Union might be moving toward something vaguely resembling a rule of law in the 1960s, forced disappearances found a new lease on life, with the rise of the 'National Security State' (NSS) under the aegis of the other global superpower.

The systems imposed by US-supported regimes in Asia and Latin America bore striking similarities to the Stalinist model. It was in Central and South America, above all, that 'disappearance' established a chilling centrality to the political events of the late Cold War period, in the 1970s and 1980s. Two of the most savage outposts of state terror anywhere in the world during this time were El Salvador and Guatemala. There, US-backed military governments waged campaigns of mass murder that killed hundreds of thousands of people. The victims were political opponents or anyone remotely suspected of 'progressive' sympathies and activities. Daylight 'disappearances' became an everyday fact of life, as Jeep Cherokees with tinted windows, piloted by death squads, scoured urban streets for suspected dissidents. Often the victims' bodies would turn up, horribly mutilated, in dump sites on the fringes of cities and villages. In thousands of other cases, captives disappeared into detention centers and torture chambers, surviving a few days, months, or years – or even occasionally being released, albeit forever scarred by this terrifying fall off the face of the earth, and the physical injuries inflicted. The terror was only slightly more restrained in the military dictatorships of the 'Southern Cone' (Brazil, Uruguay, Argentina, Chile) from the 1960s to the late 1980s. Although they killed far fewer people than the Central American wars, or the civil war in Colombia, these regimes were the ones most intimately associated with the practice of forced disappearance. In Chile, some 3,000 dissidents died, many after long periods of 'disappearance' in isolated locations; estimates for Argentina range up to ten times as high (30,000).

To a considerable and ironic degree, the use of disappearances in the Southern Cone societies reflected the growing importance of human-rights activism in the post–World War II period. It was no longer as acceptable to mow down demonstrators in the street, or kill them juridically after a show-trial, or announce their indefinite detention. Instead, their elimination had to be accomplished away from public view. 'Even before the military coup of March 1976,' wrote political scientist Kathryn Sikkink, 'international human rights pressures already influenced the Argentine military's very decision to use the practice of so-called disappearing their perceived political opponents rather than imprisoning them or executing them publicly.' After the coup, a national human rights movement began to emerge and forge contacts with the outside world. The result was a gradual erosion of the military regime's legitimacy, and of anti-democratic tendencies worldwide.

Against disappearance

In the 1980s, an international groundswell against forced disappearance took shape – largely as an outraged response to the epidemic of disappearances in the military dictatorships and death-squad states of Latin America and elsewhere. The phenomenon of forced disappearance was most pervasive in Argentina. And in that country, there was no force more significant in combating it than the Mothers of the Plaza de Mayo.

Las Madres ('the mothers') were middle- and working-class Argentine women united by their common experience of having a family member – a husband or son or daughter – 'disappeared' by the military regime that seized power amidst social chaos in 1976. Public protest against the regime was impossible for Argentine men – they would have been beaten, or disappeared themselves. But in a regime that based its social appeal on political and religious conservatism, including the Catholic idealization of the maternal figure, it would have been bad form indeed to club mothers and grandmothers to the ground. *Las Madres*, accordingly, seized their opportunity. Political activists for the first time in their lives, the women began gathering weekly in the Plaza de Mayo, the central square of Buenos Aires where the presidential palace and government ministries are clustered. The demonstrations carved out a small but highly symbolic space for popular protest, even after the state began to crack down brutally on the Mothers: three out of the fourteen founding members were disappeared. In 2005, the remains of Azucena Villaflor, one of the founders, were identified by forensic experts. Her ashes were reburied in the Plaza de Mayo that she had linked forever with the movement she helped create.

As the Mothers' activities attracted international attention, they also fired the imagination of international cultural figures, further magnifying their influence. U2's song 'Mothers of the Disappeared' closes their multimillion-selling 1987 album, *The Joshua Tree*. Sting penned 'They Dance Alone' based on the haunting image of Argentine and Chilean mothers dancing alone 'with their invisible ones' at public gatherings. Perhaps the most moving testimonial in song was that of the Panamanian singer and activist Ruben Blades, whose 'Desapariciones' (Disappearances) personalized the disappeared, describing them as the ordinary husband who owns a car-repair business; the daughter 'named Alma Gracia, just like her grandmother' who had mysteriously gone missing; the pre-med student son, surely 'a good boy'; the mother taken away – by whom, no one knew.

Cinema, too, memorably explored the theme of forced disappearances during the 1980s. The Oscar-winning Argentine film *The Official Story* (1985), made shortly after the end of military rule, touched upon one of the more macabre aspects of the political repression under the junta: the kidnapping of the children (often born in captivity) of 'disappeared' female dissidents, and their turning over to childless military couples. A more mainstream depiction was *Missing*, directed by Costa-Gavras, one of the most hard-hitting political films of the 1980s. The movie, starring Jack Lemmon and Sissy Spacek, traced the fate of Charles Horman, a young US American who had settled in Chile under the socialist regime of Salvador Allende. After the 1973 coup that led to Allende's death and the installation of a seventeen-year military dictatorship under Augusto Pinochet, Horman 'disappeared' into the custody of Chilean authorities and was never seen alive again, despite intensive efforts by his wife and father to locate him.

Efforts by Amnesty International and key state sponsors, especially from newly democratizing countries in Latin America, led in 1992 to the UN General Assembly's Declaration on the

Protection of all Persons from Enforced Disappearance. The declaration gave voice to a growing international consensus that 'enforced disappearance undermines the deepest values of any society committed to respect for the rule of law, human rights and fundamental freedoms, and that the systematic practice of

DECLARATION ON THE PROTECTION OF ALL PERSONS FROM ENFORCED DISAPPEARANCE

ARTICLE 1

- Any act of enforced disappearance is an offence to human dignity. It is condemned as a denial of the purposes of the Charter of the United Nations and as a grave and flagrant violation of the human rights and fundamental freedoms proclaimed in the Universal Declaration of Human Rights and reaffirmed and developed in international instruments in this field.
- Any act of enforced disappearance places the persons subjected thereto outside the protection of the law and inflicts severe suffering on them and their families. It constitutes a violation of the rules of international law guaranteeing, inter alia, the right to recognition as a person before the law, the right to liberty and security of the person and the right not to be subjected to torture and other cruel, inhuman or degrading treatment or punishment. It also violates or constitutes a grave threat to the right to life.

ARTICLE 2

- No State shall practice, permit or tolerate enforced disappearances.
- States shall act at the national and regional levels and in cooperation with the United Nations to contribute by all means to the prevention and eradication of enforced disappearance.

General Assembly resolution 47/133, 18 December 1992.

such acts is of the nature of a crime against humanity' (see Box on previous page).

Not surprisingly, the organization for the region chiefly afflicted by force disappearance, the Organization of American States (OAS), introduced its own 'Convention on Forced Disappearance of Persons' in 1994. It depicts forced disappearances as 'an affront to the conscience of the Hemisphere and a grave and abominable offense against the inherent dignity of the human being'.

Iraq, the 'war on terror', and the resurgence of disappearance

> Forced disappearances are not a thing of the past. They continue all over the world – in Algeria, Colombia, Nepal, the Russian Federation, Sri Lanka, the former Yugoslavia – to name but a few countries. The USA, sometimes acting with the complicity of other governments, has carried out forced disappearances of terror suspects. Those who commit these crimes have done so with almost complete impunity.
>
> Amnesty International, 2007

Since the onset of the 'war on terror' in September 2001, disappearance has paradoxically grown more visible than at any time since the military dictatorships of the 1970s and 1980s. This is evident in two main spheres. In US-occupied Iraq, the practices of the security-and-torture state, perfected under the Guatemalan or Argentine generals and indeed in Saddam Hussein's Iraq, have proliferated. Disappearances of mostly younger men, selectively or en masse, have regularly made international headlines. The detainees and death-squad victims were predominantly Sunni Muslims; their captors and executioners, predominantly Shi'ite militia members operating under the aegis (and with the immunity) of the Interior Ministry established under US patronage (see chapter 6).

Superpower policy in the 'war on terror' has likewise resumed a dimension of Night and Fog. The US has used its political and logistical clout to establish a network of so-called 'black sites' into which detainees can disappear for long periods, for CIA 'processing' and/or 'rendition'. Kidnappings on foreign territory, often with the complicity of national governments, have also featured, evoking grim memories of the abductions of perceived dissidents on the streets of Latin American cities under military rule.

The only antidote to disappearance is effective vigilance. The leading campaigners against forced disappearances – Amnesty

'I CAN'T BELIEVE THESE THINGS CAN HAPPEN . . .': NADJA DIZDAREVIC

'Dear Friends, I am so shocked by this information that it seems as if my blood froze in my veins, I can't breathe and I wish I was dead. I can't believe these things can happen, that they can come and take your husband away, overnight and without reason, destroy your family, ruin your dreams after three years of fight . . . Please, tell me, what can I still do for him? . . . Is this decision final, what are the legal remedies? Help me to understand because, as far as I know the law, this is insane, contrary to all possible laws and human rights. Please help me, I don't want to lose him.'

Dizdarevic is the wife of Hadj Boudella, a Muslim of Algerian origin living in Sarajevo, Bosnia. Boudella was arrested by Bosnian authorities and released for lack of evidence. Subsequently, CIA agents kidnapped him from his home and transported him to the US-run prison at Guantánamo Bay, Cuba. The letter was written after the Pentagon's Combatant Status Review Tribunal denied Boudella's plea for a review of his case. Quoted in Jane Mayer, 'Outsourcing Torture', *The New Yorker*, 14 February 2005.

International and Human Rights Watch – have played a stalwart role in documenting the system of 'black sites' and the experiences of those detained, disappeared, and sometimes released. Another important contribution hails from an unlikely source within civil society. This is the international network of 'planespotter' hobbyists who track the movements of individual aircraft around the world. As explained by Dana Priest in *The Washington Post*, one of the CIA-operated Gulfstream C jets used in the rendition process was unmasked by the network of spotters and bloggers, who traced its visits to 'Islamabad; Karachi; Riyadh, Saudi Arabia; Dubai; Tashkent, Uzbekistan; Baghdad; Kuwait City; Baku, Azerbaijan; and Rabat, Morocco', as well as frequent stops 'at Dulles International Airport, at Jordan's military airport in Amman and at airports in Frankfurt, Germany; Glasgow, Scotland, and Larnaca, Cyprus'.

Protests against 'extraordinary rendition' have centered on the claims of survivors, assisted by sympathizers in the legal and civil-liberties communities in the US and elsewhere. (The American Civil Liberties Union, ACLU, has played an especially prominent role.) Still, redress has been difficult to obtain. Maher Arar, a Canadian detained in the US and tortured in Syria, won a multimillion-dollar settlement from the Canadian government. In the US, however, he has been denied the right to press his claim against American authorities. The same is true of Khaled Masri, a German disappeared, imprisoned, and tortured over many months in a 'black site' run by the CIA in Afghanistan. In October 2007, the Supreme Court rejected Masri's claim for a hearing, accepting White House arguments that the need to uphold a 'state secrets privilege' overruled Masri's claim. By such means, the Bush government, even late in its tenure and amidst a Democratic resurgence in Congress, enjoyed immunity from oversight on 'national security' grounds.

Thus, just as a nascent prohibition regime against forced disappearances was gathering force, the world's leading power chose to undermine it. Nonetheless, extraordinary progress has been made in regions – notably Latin America – where disappearances were once the order of the day. In Colombia, the phenomenon is still common, and elsewhere in the hemisphere death squads roam freely (see chapter 5). As systematic state policy, though, disappearances have been marginalized through an enforcement regime effectively overseen by the Inter-American Court of Human Rights (IACHR). As so often in the human rights sphere, it is a case of two steps forward, one step back. Still, with many countries relieved of the disappearances that once plagued them, the progress seems genuine.

9
Apartheid

Apartheid (meaning 'separatehood' in the Afrikaans language) refers to the system of demographic separation and racial discrimination imposed in South Africa between 1948 and 1990. With late and marginal exceptions, the country's political sphere was reserved exclusively for South Africa's white elite, both Afrikaners of Dutch descent and British who immigrated when Britannia ruled the waves. Whites monopolized all good lands, with blacks increasingly confined to reserves (bantustans) that became spuriously independent 'homelands'. The education system was constructed to favor whites overwhelmingly; blacks were taught only what was deemed necessary for them to assume their subordinate position in an economy based on their dispossession and hyperexploitation. Above all, the apartheid system was the legislation that enshrined it, buttressed by the security forces that protected white rule against the restive African majority.

In central respects, the order imposed in South Africa in 1948 (and in the neighboring country of Namibia under South African rule) did not lack for precedents:

- In North America from the eighteenth to twentieth centuries, Native Americans were systematically attacked and corralled. When not exterminated outright, they were transported to marginal territories often hundreds of miles distant, where sickness, alcoholism, and early death were the norm. The Native American experience was paralleled by that of other indigenous peoples, including the aboriginal populations of New Zealand and Australia.

- In the US, following the end of slavery with the North's conquest of the South in the Civil War (1861–5), a pattern of so-called legislation was introduced by resurgent racist elements in the South. The aim was to cancel the political and economic gains enjoyed by some blacks during Reconstruction. What came to be known as 'Jim Crow' allowed for the basic domination and dependence at the heart of slavery to be maintained – with blacks formally free, but mostly reduced to sharecropping on white plantations (see chapter 4). Literacy tests and property requirements forced black leaders and voters out of the political system. Hundreds of terrorist lynchings of black men made it crystal-clear that impunity reigned: no state authority would protect a black to whom a crowd of whites took a fatal dislike. 'Jim Crow' was institutionalized by the principle of 'separate but equal', which excluded blacks from white-reserved facilities, confined them to their own poorly financed schools, and effectively locked them up in their own ghettoes.

- Apartheid's obsession with racial classifications and prevention of miscegenation (racial mixing through sexual relations) echoed the preoccupation of eugenics theorists in the US and UK, who sought to manage reproductive patterns as a means to improve the overall physical and mental health of a population, and the Nazi totalitarians who seized power in Germany in 1933. The influence of National Socialism (Nazism) on National Party ideology in South Africa was extensive; the Nationalists took power in Pretoria in the same decade that had seen the Nazis ascendant, albeit briefly, throughout Europe. For the Nazis, 'contamination' of Aryan (Nordic) blood by 'inferior races' – above all, Jews – was a crime punishable by death. The apartheid system was less tightly controlled, and many African women were sexually exploited by white men. But 'purity of blood' – welded to a

brutally efficient security apparatus – was the heart of both
the Nazi and the apartheid systems.

Within South Africa itself, there were precedents for apartheid
so obvious as to make 1948 seem more of a culmination than a
revolution. A substantial degree of racial mixing followed British
colonization of the Cape Colony around present-day Cape
Town. This scandalized descendants of the original white
settlers, the Boer farmer class, which also chafed under restric-
tions on the use of African labor after Britain abolished slavery
throughout the Empire. The year of the abolition was 1833; by
1838, Afrikaners were streaming east in the 'Great Trek' by
which they conquered the interior of present-day South Africa.

Only the British were powerful enough to displace the Boers
in the territories they claimed – and a motherlode of gold and
diamonds, discovered in the 1870s and 1880s, gave them a
mighty incentive to do so. The Boer War of 1899–1902 crushed
Afrikaner resistance; but the Afrikaners' spirited guerrilla struggle sparked sympathy even in England, and the peace imposed
was generous. The signal Land Act legislation of 1913, together
with other discriminatory measures against the black and colored
(mixed-race) population and their continued denial of political
rights, represented concessions to Boer racism and fears of
economic marginalization. Politically, Afrikanerdom was
allowed to regroup under British hegemony. The waning of the
British empire with the end of World War II offered an oppor-
tune moment for the Afrikaners' main political vehicle, the
National Party, to take power.

The system of apartheid instituted after 1948 can be under-
stood as the product of both top-down and bottom-up initiatives. The elite aspect is more familiar: Afrikaner politicians
increasingly saw the strict management of race relations as essential to the community's survival, and as a path to entrenching the
Afrikaner political class in power indefinitely. The Dutch

Reformed Church preached racial inequality and separation to its flock, which included the politicians with whom it collaborated in shaping and supporting apartheid policies. The mysterious *Broederbond* (Brotherhood), a secret organization of some 12,000 members, provided the glue for disparate elements of the Afrikaner elite. It was 'perhaps unequalled in the world for its pervasive back-room power wielded over nearly every aspect of national life'.

At the same time, however, apartheid offered working-class Afrikaners a powerful stake in the system – one they shared with *all* whites, while 'coloreds' of mostly Indian descent occupied an intermediate position. As long as apartheid existed, whites would dominate the economic hierarchy, bolstered by the apparatus of a highly interventionist state. However far down the ladder they might be compared to other whites, they would enjoy rights that *no* black person in the country did. They would exert an authority in both occupational and social spheres that would be unthinkable were they forced to compete on market terms with cheaper, more widely available black labor.

The apartheid state

Racial 'separatehood' in power and in practice was constructed around two key laws: the Group Areas Act of 1950 and the Separate Amenities Act of 1953. The former was the cornerstone of 'grand apartheid' – the vision of a South African population confined to its various national territories, with eighty-seven percent of the land reserved for whites (including all prime real estate and known natural resources). The Separate Amenities Act echoed the segregation system in the southern US, reserving educational, medical, and recreational facilities for whites and nonwhites, with the latter predictably starved of state attention and investment.

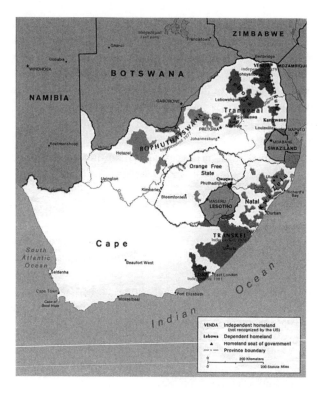

Figure 6 Map of apartheid-era South Africa, showing the Black 'homelands' (such as Transkei and Bophuthatswana) created on barren territories to provide an illusion of African political autonomy.

Racial 'mixing', in both a sexual and a social sense, was formally banned or strictly regulated. All political opposition, beyond a small liberal fringe anchored in the English white community, was stamped out under the Suppression of Communism Act (1950), in which 'communism' served as code for any movement favoring majority rights and rule. Beginning in the mid 1950s, the core institution of 'grand apartheid' was inaugurated with the eviction of blacks from settlements in white-designated lands, and their relocation to the barren 'homelands'. (So notorious did the 'homelands' policy become in the outside world that millions of activist-inclined Westerners actually learned to pronounce 'Bophuthatswana', one of the ten entities created to provide a façade of political autonomy for blacks, while maintaining all real power in white hands – see figure 6.)

'WE WANT EQUAL POLITICAL RIGHTS': NELSON MANDELA (1964)

Africans want to be paid a living wage. Africans want to perform work which they are capable of doing, and not work which the government declares them to be capable of. Africans want to be allowed to live where they obtain work, and not be endorsed out of [evicted from] an area because they were not born there. Africans want to be allowed to own land in places where they work, and not to be obliged to live in rented houses which they can never call their own. Africans want to be part of the general population, and not confined to living in their own ghettoes. African men want to have their wives and children to live with them where they work, and not be forced into an unnatural existence in men's hostels. African women want to be with their menfolk and not be left permanently widowed in the Reserves. Africans want to be allowed out after eleven o'clock at night and not to be confined to their rooms like little children. Africans want to be allowed to travel in their own country and to seek work where they want to and not where the Labor Bureau tells them to. Africans want a just share in the whole of South Africa; they want security and a stake in society. Above all, we want equal political rights, because without them our disabilities will be permanent . . .

Second Court Statement in the Rivonia Trial of Mandela and nine others, 20 April 1964; in *Nelson Mandela: The Struggle is My Life* (New York: Pathfinder Press, 1986), p. 168.

Black resistance was decimated and driven underground. Still, it simmered throughout the 1950s and into the 1960s, led by the African National Congress (ANC), originally founded in 1912 to oppose the discriminatory Land Act legislation. The Sharpeville Massacre of 1960, in which dozens of Africans protesting pass laws were shot to death by police, prompted the ANC to establish an armed wing, *Umkhonto we Sizwe* ('Spear of the Nation'). A relatively small-scale sabotage campaign followed. It gave the authorities the excuse they needed to impose a state of emergency and round up most of the underground leadership. ANC leader Nelson Mandela and seven others were sentenced to life in prison at the Rivonia trials of 1963–4.

The world responds: the Apartheid Convention and beyond

The International Convention on the Suppression and Punishment of the Crime of Apartheid, opened to UN member states for signature in November 1973, principally sought to condemn South African apartheid and denounce it as a Western colonial vestige. The cause was explicitly linked to the decolonization process of the post-World War II era: as part of this 'irresistible and irreversible' liberation movement, 'colonialism and all practices of segregation and discrimination associated therewith' were now anathema. According to Steven Ratner and Jason Abrams, 'The Convention was drafted hastily and was clearly meant to apply to one state alone', but an effort was made to extend its applicability beyond South Africa, by outlawing a range of destructive and persecutory measures inflicted on racial grounds. The measures included the 'crime of crimes' – genocide. In fact, the Apartheid Convention (see Box opposite) explicitly echoed the language of the Genocide Convention, referring to 'the infliction upon the members of a racial group or groups of serious bodily or mental harm' and 'deliberate imposition on a racial group or groups of living conditions calculated to cause its or their physical destruction in whole or in part'. However, it also stressed measures such as imposing discriminatory legislation and unjust conditions of work upon a racial group.

Issued just prior to the last great surge of decolonization (Portugal's surrender of its African colonies in 1975), the Convention was designed as a means for the international community to place its seal on the growing opposition to South African apartheid, and thereby speed its demise. This opposition had spread around the globe, beginning perhaps with British Prime Minister Harold MacMillan's 'Wind of Change' speech in February 1960, which acknowledged the 'growth of national consciousness' among the world's colonized peoples as 'a political fact'. Delivered to the South African parliament, MacMillan's address was followed, in 1961, by South Africa's proclamation as a republic and its withdrawal from the British Commonwealth.

INTERNATIONAL CONVENTION ON THE SUPPRESSION AND PUNISHMENT OF THE CRIME OF APARTHEID (30 NOVEMBER 1973): ARTICLE II

For the purpose of the present Convention, the term 'the crime of apartheid', which shall include similar policies and practices of racial segregation and discrimination as practised in southern Africa, shall apply to the following inhuman acts committed for the purpose of establishing and maintaining domination by one racial group of persons over any other racial group of persons and systematically oppressing them:

(a) Denial to a member or members of a racial group or groups of the right to life and liberty of person:

    (i) By murder of members of a racial group or groups;

    (ii) By the infliction upon the members of a racial group or

> ## INTERNATIONAL CONVENTION ON THE SUPPRESSION AND PUNISHMENT OF THE CRIME OF APARTHEID (*cont.*)
>
> groups of serious bodily or mental harm, by the infringement of their freedom or dignity, or by subjecting them to torture or to cruel, inhuman or degrading treatment or punishment;
>
> (iii) By arbitrary arrest and illegal imprisonment of the members of a racial group or groups;
>
> (b) Deliberate imposition on a racial group or groups of living conditions calculated to cause its or their physical destruction in whole or in part;
>
> (c) Any legislative measures and other measures calculated to prevent a racial group or groups from participation in the political, social, economic, and cultural life of the country and the deliberate creation of conditions preventing the full development of such a group or groups, in particular by denying to members of a racial group or groups basic human rights and freedoms . . .
>
> (d) Any measures, including legislative measures, designed to divide the population along racial lines by the creation of separate reserves and ghettos for the members of a racial group or groups, the prohibition of mixed marriages among members of various racial groups, the expropriation of landed property belonging to a racial group or groups or to members thereof;
>
> (e) Exploitation of the labor of the members of a racial group or groups, in particular by submitting them to forced labor;
>
> (f) Persecution of organizations and persons, by depriving them of fundamental rights and freedoms, because they oppose apartheid.

At the state level, however, international opposition to apartheid in the 1970s and 1980s was diffuse and inchoate, at least among those nations best positioned to affect events. The policy was hamstrung by mixed motives, reflecting South Africa's perceived importance as a source of strategic minerals and a bulwark against communist expansion in Africa. Most Western leaders proved ready to wag fingers, but reluctant to move beyond what the US government dubbed 'constructive engagement'. With South Africa under an almost constant state of emergency, and the Cold War apparently at its height, few Western governments wished to press the apartheid regime further.

A number of international factors contributed to the final collapse of South African apartheid. A decade earlier, white rule had collapsed next door in Rhodesia, and an independent black-ruled Zimbabwe had come into being. South Africa's military expansionism beyond its Namibian colony into Angola was decisively checked at the Battle of Cuito Cuanavale in 1988 (with Cuban fighters shoring up Angolan liberation forces). The advent of *glasnost* and *perestroika* – 'openness' and 'restructuring' – under Mikhail Gorbachev in the communist Soviet Union began to thaw superpower relations, and undermine the Cold War mentality of 'Total Onslaught' that the Nationalist government had relied on to justify its hold on power.

Economic and cultural sanctions had also begun to bite, sapping the will and increasing the sense of siege among South Africa's white minority. The anti-apartheid movement had captured imaginations and activist energies in Western countries, especially on university campuses. The movement pushed for divestment from South African holdings; staged substantial demonstrations; and picketed international appearances by South African political figures and sports teams.

Opposition on the cultural front was also highly visible – and audible. In South Africa, the vocal group Ladysmith Black Mambazo established itself as the voice of Soweto, the sprawling township that became synonymous with the apartheid order. Lucky Dube pushed the limits of apartheid censorship with songs such as 'Together as One' ('Too many people / Hate apartheid/Why do you like it?'). Artists in exile, such as Miriam Makeba and Hugh Masekela, served as touring representatives of the liberation movement. Song was also important to mobilizations in the countries of the West. Paul Simon arranged for Ladysmith Black Mambazo to appear on his 1986 album *Graceland*, which included a haunting a cappella song titled 'Homeless'. The album sold 14 million copies. Less ubiquitous, but more politically aggressive, was the Artists United Against Apartheid initiative, launched by Little Steven Van Zandt of Bruce Springsteen's E-Street band. Van Zandt organized a boycott of the Sun City entertainment resort in the apartheid 'homeland' of Bophuthatswana. Many international stars, including Queen, Julio Iglesias, and Rod Stewart, were lured by large payouts to play concerts at Sun City – and by extension to legitimize the 'homelands' policy. Van Zandt's song declared in protest: 'I ain't gonna play Sun City'; a couple of dozen of rock's biggest acts, including Springsteen and the ubiquitous Bono of U2, lent their voices to the recording.

With the liberation movement a seemingly unstoppable force, global opinion volubly supporting it, and the Cold War drawing to a close, South African President F. W. de Klerk took decisive steps to dismantle apartheid as traditionally conceived. In February 1990, he freed Nelson Mandela and other political prisoners, and abolished most of the 'petty apartheid' measures – 'Whites Only' signs in public places, and so on – that had outraged liberal sensitivities at home and abroad. De Klerk aimed to install a new order that would accord the white minority a veto over key legislation, but the momentum of the transformations, and a pervasive climate of violence, made such 'compromise' unfeasible. On 27 April 1994, millions of blacks, whites, coloreds, and ethnic Indians lined up for the first free polls in South African history. The African National Congress, leader of the liberation struggle, crushed all opposition, but pledged to rule as far as possible by consensus.

The result, in the eyes of many critics, was the perpetuation of key elements of the former system. Disparities between majority and minority populations were only partly offset by the rise of a black political and entrepreneurial class, which promptly abandoned the townships and moved into the gated, high-walled suburbs formerly occupied by whites exclusively. Nonetheless, apartheid as such had been decisively obliterated. It remained for other peoples – Palestinians, women, the global poor – to take up the term as a mobilizing tool for their own struggles.

Israeli apartheid?

Beyond its colonial South African roots, 'apartheid' has been applied as a pejorative most prominently in the case of the Israeli-occupied West Bank, seized in the 1967 Six-Day War. Resolutions depicting Israel as an 'apartheid state' were a regular feature at the World Conference Against Racism in Durban, South Africa, in 2001. In 2002, two prominent figures in the South African liberation struggle, Desmond Tutu and Ian Urbina, published a declaration 'Against Israeli Apartheid'. 'Yesterday's South African township dwellers can tell you about today's life in the occupied territories. To travel only blocks in his own homeland, a grandfather waits on the whim of a teenage soldier . . . The indignities, dependence and anger are all too familiar.' With former US President Jimmy Carter's 2006 book, *Palestine: Peace Not Apartheid*, the analogy's deployment sparked widespread controversy (see Box overleaf).

The construction of a wall or, as the Israeli government referred to it, a 'security fence' running for much of the length of the West Bank, carried great symbolic weight. It was under construction at the time of writing – ostensibly to prevent terrorists reaching the Jewish heartland, but also to

APARTHEID IN PALESTINE?: JIMMY CARTER

Palestine: Peace Not Apartheid is devoted to circumstances and events in Palestine and not in Israel, where democracy prevails and citizens live together and are legally guaranteed equal status . . . The book describes the abominable oppression and persecution in the occupied Palestinian territories, with a rigid system of required passes and strict segregation between Palestine's citizens and Jewish settlers in the West Bank. An enormous imprisonment wall is now under construction, snaking through what is left of Palestine, to encompass more and more land for Israeli settlers. In many ways, this is more oppressive than what black people lived under in South Africa during apartheid. I have made it clear that the motivation is not racism but the desire of a minority of Israelis to confiscate and colonise choice sites in Palestine, and then to forcefully suppress any objections from the displaced citizens.

Jimmy Carter, 'Israel, Palestine, peace and apartheid',
the *Guardian*, 12 December 2006.

divide Palestinian communities, and isolate them from the territories, especially around Jerusalem and in the Jordan Valley, that Israel sought to retain in a negotiated settlement. The parallels with the dispossession of the black population of South Africa, beginning (in the modern era) with the Land Act of 1913 and continuing through the grim 'homelands' policy, were further fuel for Carter and other critics of the Israeli occupation.

The Israeli occupation regime also shared with South African apartheid a range of 'security' procedures that imposed onerous burdens and daily humiliations on the Palestinian population. Palestinians were hemmed in at every turn, or penned like cattle in security tunnels for hours under Israeli military vigilance when they sought to leave their home areas. The Israelis dictated that Palestinians dig wells only a third as deep as those of Jewish settlers on their territory: an apt symbol of the infantilizing of the subject population, and another parallel legitimately drawn with South African apartheid.

Important differences between the two systems were also evident, however. In a measured review of *Palestine: Peace Not Apartheid*, Joseph Lelyveld – a longtime correspondent in apartheid-era South Africa – argued that there was nothing 'remotely resembling the apartheid doctrine or apparatus . . . within Israel itself'. Moreover, 'Israel has proven that it's not at all dependent on imported cheap labor from the [occupied] territories', while South Africa would have collapsed economically without black labor from the 'homelands'. Nonetheless, Lelyveld conceded that 'significant similarities can be found in the occupation of the territories' and the apartheid system.

Global apartheid

The elements of subjugation and exploitation that pervaded South African apartheid made the label an attractive one for activists in other issue-areas who were seeking to engage in 'norm grafting'. Hence the advent of the term 'global apartheid', to convey the inequality inherent in relations between the wealthier societies of the world and the poorer ones. The phrase seems to have been used first by international relations scholar Gernot Kohler in 1978, then expanded upon by Titus Alexander in a 1996 book, *Unraveling Global Apartheid*. Figures such as South African President Thabo Mbeki and Cuban President Fidel Castro have also employed it.

In the summary of Salih Booker and William Minter of the NGO Africa Action, global apartheid 'is an international system of minority rule whose attributes include: differential access to basic human rights; wealth and power structured by race and place; structural racism, embedded in global economic processes, political institutions and cultural assumptions; and the international practice of double standards that assume inferior rights to be appropriate for certain "others", defined by location, origin, race or gender'. Booker and Minter express a conviction that global apartheid 'is more than a metaphor'. Control over the labor and resources of the world's subordinate populations is 'far more complex and differentiated than the apartheid system in South Africa'. But the 'resulting global inequality', they argue, is even greater than the extremes that prevailed under South African apartheid.

In his book *Unravelling Global Apartheid*, Alexander also stresses that no straightforward equation is possible between global apartheid and the South African variant. Among other things, 'the West is not a unitary state', and cannot be approached as an undifferentiated entity. As well, the West's exercise of domination through a system of global apartheid – the fundamental 'inequality between the West and the world's majority' – does not rely upon an explicitly racist ideology or racially discriminatory policies. Race is just one of the variables – including social class and gender – that position individuals in the global system. What is common to both systems, apart from their origins in colonialism and structural dependency, is the fundamental, dramatically unequal, and de facto racialized relations at their core. The explicitness of racial discrimination in South African apartheid was eventually too much for a cosmopolitan conscience to bear. Apartheid ended by being 'almost universally condemned . . . declared a crime in international law and made subject to boycotts by most countries of the world'. But the parallel inequality in relations between a global (white-dominated) North and global (non-white) South, argues Titus, 'rarely arouses similar indignation or political action, although it is just as immoral and illegitimate. It deserves the same condemnation.'

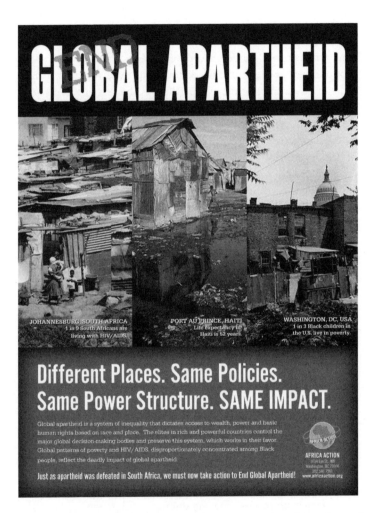

Figure 7 Global apartheid. (Courtesy Africa Action, www.africaaction.org)

Gender apartheid

The concept of 'gender apartheid' seems first to have been propounded as a means of denouncing Afghanistan's former Taliban government. Just as 'apartheid is the "strict racial segregation as practiced in South Africa,"' wrote one NGO, so 'gender apartheid has been used to describe the strict gender-based segregation . . . practiced in Afghanistan.' Indeed, the kind of micro-control and (at least initially) total exclusion from economic and social life for Afghan women far exceeded anything imposed on black South Africans (see Box below).

The invasion and occupation of Afghanistan in 2001 overthrew the Taliban regime, expelling surviving leaders and

---

GENDER APARTHEID IN AFGHANISTAN: FEMINIST MAJORITY FOUNDATION

When they took control in 1996, the Taliban initially imposed strict edicts that:

- Banished women from the work force
- Closed schools to girls in cities and expelled women from universities
- Prohibited women from leaving their homes unless accompanied by a close male relative
- Ordered the publicly visible windows of women's houses painted black and forced women to wear the burqa (or chadari) – which completely shrouds the body, leaving only a small mesh-covered opening through which to see
- Prohibited women and girls from being examined by male physicians while at the same time, prohibited most female doctors and nurses from working.

Taken from www.feminist.org/afghan/facts.html

rank–and–file militants to Pakistan. From there, they launched increasingly ferocious cross–border raids against Afghan and foreign troops and civilians. In areas of the country that they managed to reconquer, the Taliban made it clear that their fundamentalist interpretation of women's place in a theocratic society had not changed. Meanwhile, their main competitors for power in Afghanistan, the warlords whom the Taliban had usurped in 1996, often seemed scarcely less medieval in their outlook.

Gender apartheid extends beyond Afghanistan to other parts of the Muslim world. In Saudi Arabia, for example, women are forbidden to drive or vote, and are visually segregated behind restrictive burqas. Facilities for education, worship, and work are strictly segregated, along with many other public and social settings. Women's public roles are broader in fundamentalist-controlled Iran, but segregation is still extensive, and religious police roam the streets, beating and arresting women who fail to abide by strict dress codes.

The status, or rather lack of it, of women in the global order also prompts comparisons with apartheid. Women's labor, like that of South Africa's blacks in the apartheid era, is undervalued and underpaid. Women historically have been held in reserve, to be drawn into the public sphere at moments of political crisis or labor need, and otherwise consigned to the domestic realm (the home/'homeland') where their rights and personal potential are heavily constrained. Moreover, sexist ideologies in many ways parallel racist ones. They depict women as inferior, limited by nature to particular life roles, and ever dependent on paternalistic guidance and sustenance.

The human toll exacted by sexist ideologies is enormous, far exceeding the destructive impact of racial apartheid and similar practices. Female infanticide has killed tens of millions of children throughout history. Female fetuses, when identified by ultrasound tests, are vastly more prone than male ones to be aborted in some Asian countries, notably India and China. Girls'

educational and nutritional deficits are 'widespread or systematic' in many countries of the global South. All of these crimes
are inflicted upon females before they even reach adolescence –
if they ever do.

As these examples show, the main purpose of extending the
apartheid framing beyond the South African context is to engage
in 'norm grafting'. If racialized, unequal power relations were
unacceptable in the national context of South Africa, why are
they taken for granted at a global level? If separation and
discrimination on the basis of race are illegitimate, why should
they be permitted on grounds of gender? 'Global apartheid' and
'gender apartheid' activists seek to utilize some of the moral
authority that attaches to the anti-apartheid struggle to legitimize
their own cause. They do not expect that inequalities of gender
and economic class will be prosecuted under the Apartheid
Convention. But they use the concept to point to pervasive and
deeply entrenched patterns of domination and exploitation, and
illuminate important connections between the national and the
global.

Such activism also reminds us that apartheid exerted a
powerful pull over ordinary members of the dominant society.
South African whites often found it easy to accommodate
themselves to a manifestly unjust system, because they benefited
so appreciably by it. Israeli settlers in the West Bank are often
drawn less by religious zealotry than by the chance to live a
heavily subsidized existence in a California-style subdivision,
within easy commuting distance of Israel's major cities. So it is
with less event-specific and timebound forms of apartheid –
those that have spread and congealed into global institutions. In
a significant sense, most readers of this book have a stake in
systems of structural inequality and discrimination. Most must
transcend their allegiances as comparatively privileged members
of the global order, if they are to play a role in undermining the
injustices that pervade it.

Conclusion

The future of crimes against humanity

The human landscape sometimes seems so bleak as to hardly justify efforts to brighten it. We confront crises, looming or pervasive, on a dizzying number of fronts. As I drafted these pages, media reports described unprecedentedly severe droughts and floods in diverse parts of the world; epidemic disease, genocide, and mass rape in Africa; wild rollercoaster rides on international financial markets; deep instability in nuclear-armed Pakistan . . . As individuals, we may feel like the Dutch boy with his finger in the dike – except that new leaks are always springing up beyond our reach; others' ability or willingness to help is uncertain; and even where we stand, the hole appears too big for our trivial efforts to plug it. The content of this book – its presentation of so much atrocity in distilled form – may reinforce feelings of paralysis and apathy. Why not simply retreat and 'cultivate one's garden', as Voltaire's Candide chose to do?

One reason to engage with the challenges before us is that this is far from the first time that humanity has confronted severe crisis and widespread atrocity. The world must have looked similar to the generation in the West that emerged from the desperate years of the Great Depression, only to find themselves swept up in history's worst war. Yet the over-mythologized 'Greatest Generation' responded with the biggest wave of human rights institution-building ever known, and with a peace that was one of the most protracted ever recorded among the great powers.

Among that generation's projects was the entrenching of an idea of 'crimes against humanity' in international law. The core concept was one of a human collective, linked by common cognitive, social, and spiritual capacities. This collective is something that every individual partakes of, deriving some of his or her identity from it. The proper posture toward 'humanity', these architects and activists declared, is respect, protection, and succor. An integral part of the contemporary human project is the growing extensiveness and practical inclusiveness of this communal vision.

Thus, the fact that a concept of 'crimes against humanity' exists at all, and that you have been motivated (or assigned) to pick up this book and read it, suggests that humanity has managed to articulate something essential about its vulnerable condition, and the moral imperative to protect it. Such notions have inspired committed individuals for centuries.

Examples of these efforts appear regularly in these pages. They are manifest in the declarations of those, like Olaudah Equiano and Raphael Lemkin, who spoke on behalf of populations trampled by slavery and genocide. They include the ordinary letter-writers and placard-wielders of the Anti-Slavery Society and Amnesty International. They are the UN personnel who refused evacuation from Dili, East Timor, while refugees sheltering in the UN compound were at risk of murder by paramilitary thugs roaming outside. Indeed, we arrive at this conclusion fresh from considering South African apartheid, and its end – one of the past century's towering examples of a people attaining liberation from oppression and humiliation, partial though the liberation may be. The anti-apartheid movement's sanctions campaigns and other activist strategies stand as models of their kind.

The growing momentum of these social movements and international 'principled-issue networks' attests to the erosion of one of the foundational norms of the modern period: that of uncontested state sovereignty. For centuries, the system that still organizes our world today relied upon mutual recognition of states' near-absolute right to do what they liked on their 'own' turf, and to their 'own' people. When this norm was challenged, it was usually by religious believers protesting or otherwise opposing the violent repression of coreligionists.

It took the advent of a modern, globalized world, linked by mass communications, to extend the imagination of the human community beyond the boundaries of religion and tribe. And it took multifaceted, prolonged struggles by diverse actors – including workers, women, the colonized, and ethnic minorities – to restrain the authoritarian state and institute meaningful social and civil protections at home. Norm entrepreneurs, from vanguard states and political leaders to nongovernmental organizations and ordinary individuals, then 'marketed' and 'sold' values such as equality and human rights to the wider world. Often their struggles were undermined by self-interest or paternalism; often the noblest initiatives were only partly successful. But evident throughout this book is humanity's overall capacity to confront and marginalize – even effectively banish – some of its darkest and most destructive practices.

The postwar evolution of a prohibition regime against 'crimes against humanity' is an essential aspect of this centuries-old process. There is a direct line of descent from the eighteenth-century preachers declaiming against slavery and the Caribbean slaves rising up against it, to those challenging crimes against humanity today and fighting to resist them. In just the last few years, impressive advances have been made. Take one example: the rapid undermining of the impunity granted to political leaders for atrocities committed on their watch. Until very recently, this impunity had no statute of limitations, and guaranteed many a dictator a comfortable retirement. Nascent challenges to the norm, however, were mounted as early as the trials of Ottoman figures after World War I. The Nuremberg tribunal, the Universal Declaration of Human Rights, and the UN Genocide Convention (chapters 1–2) challenged it more fundamentally still. It was not until late in the millennium – 1997, to be precise – that a retired military dictator was arrested on foreign soil for alleged involvement in crimes against humanity. The case of Augusto Pinochet transfixed the world, as the former Chilean general, coup leader, and president was accused of torturing and 'disappearing' civilian opponents. There seemed a real prospect that Pinochet would be dispatched to Spain, to stand trial for atrocities committed against Spanish citizens in Chile. In the end, the British government lifted his house arrest on 'compassionate' grounds. The octogenarian Pinochet was allowed to return to Chile, where he outlasted national efforts to prosecute him until his death in December 2006, aged 91. Later that same month, however, another dictator was dispatched more brutally. Former Iraqi president Saddam Hussein died in a hangman's noose, and trials of his henchmen are ongoing. Finally, former Peruvian leader Alberto Fujimori is in the dock in Lima as these words are written, extradited from Chile and charged with organizing death-squads to assassinate political opponents.

While out-of-power dictators make easy targets, cracks were also appearing in the façade of unthinkability surrounding trials of 'democratic' leaders. Both the former US Secretary of State Henry Kissinger, and Donald Rumsfeld, Defense Secretary in the Bush administration during the period of Abu Ghraib and other abuses, were known to be avoiding speaking engagements in countries and settings where they might be vulnerable to arrest and prosecution – or merely to embarrassing public protests.

For the individuals, whether leaders or 'ordinary' men and women, who face tribunals such as the new International Criminal Court, crimes against humanity are increasingly likely to appear on the charge-sheet. When the atrocities alleged move beyond war crimes, the attraction to prosecutors of a crimes-against-humanity framing is considerable. This is especially so when the alternative is prosecution for the crime of genocide. The crimes against humanity of 'murder', 'extermination', and 'persecution' cover much the same terrain as genocide, and a conviction results in much the same prison sentence. Proving crimes against humanity, however, does not require that a prosecutor show the acts were committed *with intent to destroy* a national, ethnic, racial, or religious group, in whole or in part. It is only required that the acts be directed against a civilian population, and be 'systematic', 'widespread', or both. Case law, notably that of the ad hoc tribunals for former Yugoslavia and Rwanda, increasingly demonstrates the difficulty of securing convictions for genocide. As a result, prosecutions for crimes against humanity may hold increasing appeal.

Another advantage of a crimes against humanity framing lies in the phrase 'and other inhumane acts', appended to the core legal understanding of such crimes in the Rome Statute of the ICC. This was instituted with the specific desire to keep the concept open and flexible, both to new forms of atrocity, and to newly restrictive postures toward established practices. In instances such as torture or rape and sexual crimes, 'crimes against humanity' has become the preferred interpretive framework for acts that were long widely accepted, even institutionalized; they are now recast as fundamental violations of human rights and integrity. In yet other cases, existing crimes against humanity have been expanded to incorporate new dimensions and manifestations, as the norm against slavery was grafted onto a concept of 'sexual enslavement'.

Still, one must be careful to avoid legal fetishism – the conviction that law is the be-all and end-all. Law has been an important arena of contestation for opponents of crimes against humanity – but only *one* such arena. As with genocide, the concept of crimes against humanity resonates far beyond the trial chamber: both as a 'catalyzing idea' in public affairs, and as a buttress for a cosmopolitan global order.

'Genocide' is one of the most powerful words in the English language. By comparison, 'crimes against humanity' has a more pedestrian, less politically charged tenor. Perhaps it seems a clumsier concept, or too abstract. But a moment's thought suggests that 'crimes against humanity' is no less potent than 'genocide', and perhaps even more capable of mobilizing humanitarian concern and intervention. The term implies that a cosmopolitan collectivity – humanity – exists, and can be criminally abused. It speaks to the claim that the Other is justified in making upon the Self, in implicit recognition that Self and Other are mutually constitutive. As a concept, 'crimes against humanity' contains the seed and contours of a prohibition regime against it – something that is true of very few catalyzing ideas.

Its potential to generate intervention marks 'crimes against humanity' as an important framework for future activist mobilizations. Might it also offer grounds for *unwarranted* intervention? Over half a century ago, Joseph Dautricourt cited the argument of Henri Donnedieu de Vabres, a French legal expert and member of the Nuremberg tribunal, that 'the theory of crimes against humanity is dangerous; dangerous for the peoples by the absence of precise definition; dangerous for the States because it offers a pretext to intervention by a State, in the internal affairs of weaker states.' Nearly fifty years later, scholar David Chandler expressed a similar concern that 'In the Middle East, in Africa and the Balkans, the exercise of "international justice" signifies a return to . . . open great-power domination over states which are too weak to prevent external claims against them.'

It would be futile to deny that a humanitarian veneer has been applied to some massively destructive and destabilizing interventions – as with Iraq in 2003. Whatever the successes in taming and eroding authoritarianism and mass atrocity in recent centuries, the underpinnings of the state system remain, and are even strengthened in an age of globalization and 'war on terror'. But the global superpower, and nation-states as a bloc, are far from the only actors in world affairs. The interventions required in coming years are not the timebound and event-specific ones – or not *only* those. They are also the structural interventions needed to confront the various acts we designate as crimes against humanity, along with the daunting profusion of other challenges that exist and impend. These interventions will be implemented by the concerted action of hundreds of millions of human beings, or they will not be implemented.

I offer no pat formulas to guide the engagement with our possible futures, except an obvious one: as goes 'humanity', so will go the crimes against it. The challenge is to transcend our tribal selves, and to imbue our cosmopolitan identities with real form and color. If we succeed in this project, then the revulsion we feel toward the current range of crimes against humanity, and that we come to feel toward 'other inhumane acts', will lead us to consign them to the margins, as with international slavery – or to the ash-heap of history, as with South African apartheid. The same transcendence of our parochial selves may help us to extend our custodianship to the natural world we inhabit. That world may then grant us an environment capable of sustaining the more humane order we seek.

Make it so.

Further reading

Note: All references and sources can be found online at
www.crimesagainsthumanity.ca

Chapter 1 – Genesis

Jonathan Glover, *Humanity: A Moral History of the Twentieth Century*.
New Haven, CT: Yale University Press, 1999. Searching exploration, a decade in the writing, of crimes against humanity and their
psychological and sociological underpinnings.

Lynn Hunt, *Inventing Human Rights: A History*. New York: W. W.
Norton & Co., 2007. Engaging account of the rise of human rights
ideals.

Margaret E. Keck and Kathryn Sikkink, *Activists Beyond Borders:
Advocacy Networks in International Politics*. Ithaca, NY: Cornell
University Press, 1998. The foundational text on norms and activist
networks in international politics.

Ethan A. Nadelmann, 'Global Prohibition Regimes: The Evolution of
Norms in International Society', *International Organization*, 44: 4
(1990), pp. 479–526. Coined the term 'prohibition regimes' and
explores their evolution.

The following books examine crimes against humanity from a legal
and/or philosophical perspective, often as part of a broader exami-
nation of humanitarian law:

M. Cherif Bassiouni, *Crimes Against Humanity in International Criminal
Law*, 2nd rev. edn. The Hague: Kluwer Law International, 1999.
Exhaustive legal survey.

Machteld Boot, *Genocide, Crimes Against Humanity, War Crimes:
Nullum Crimen Sine Lege and the Subject Matter Jurisdiction of the*

International Criminal Court. Antwerpen: Intersentia, 2002. One of the most useful specialist treatments, though hard to find.

Larry May, *Crimes Against Humanity: A Normative Account*. Cambridge: Cambridge University Press, 2005. Philosophical exploration of mass crimes and questions of individual responsibility.

Steven R. Ratner and Jason S. Abrams, *Accountability for Human Rights Atrocities in International Law: Beyond the Nuremberg Legacy*, 2nd edn. Oxford: Oxford University Press, 2001. Popular legal textbook.

Geoffrey Robertson, QC, *Crimes Against Humanity: The Struggle for Global Justice*. New York: The New Press, 2000. Lively, well-written overview of the evolution of key concepts of human rights and international law.

Chapter 2 – Genocide and extermination

Adam Jones, ed., *Genocide: A Comprehensive Introduction*. London: Routledge, 2006. My take on the subject.

Ben Kiernan, *Blood and Soil: Genocide and Extermination from Sparta to Darfur*. New Haven, CT: Yale University Press, 2007. Magnum opus by the director of Yale University's Genocide Studies Program.

Leo Kuper, *Genocide: Its Political Use in the Twentieth Century*. Harmondsworth: Penguin, 1981. The field-defining work of genocide studies.

Mark Levene, *Genocide in the Age of the Nation-State* (2 vols). Oxford: Oxford University Press, 2005. Wonderfully stimulating historical and theoretical analysis.

Martin Shaw, *What Is Genocide?* Cambridge: Polity, 2006. Concise and richly insightful.

Chapter 3 – Forced population transfer and 'ethnic cleansing'

Bruce Clark, *Twice a Stranger: The Mass Expulsions that Forged Modern Greece and Turkey*. Cambridge, MA: Harvard University Press, 2006.

Highly readable account of the forced population transfers following World War I.

Michael Ignatieff, *Blood and Belonging: Journeys into the New Nationalism*. Toronto: Viking, 1993. The resurgence of ethnicity as a political force, in Europe and elsewhere.

Benjamin Lieberman, *Terrible Fate: Ethnic Cleansing in the Making of Modern Europe*. Chicago, IL: Ivan R. Dee, 2006. Wideranging account of the role of 'cleansing' practices, from the nineteenth century to the present.

Norman M. Naimark, *Fires of Hatred: Ethnic Cleansing in Twentieth-Century Europe*. Cambridge, MA: Harvard University Press, 2001. Another solid treatment with a European focus.

Ilan Pappe, *The Ethnic Cleansing of Palestine*. Oxford: Oneworld Publications, 2006. Examines Israel's killing and expulsion of Palestinians in 1948 as a paradigmatic instance of 'cleansing'.

Alfred-Maurice de Zayas, *A Terrible Revenge: The Ethnic Cleansing of the East European Germans*. London: Palgrave Macmillan, 1994. Concise study of the mass expulsions and large-scale killing of ethnic Germans at the war's end.

Chapter 4 – Slavery and human trafficking

David Batstone, *Not for Sale: The Return of the Global Slave Trade – and How We Can Fight It*. New York: Harper, 2007. Despite the hyperbolic title, an important exposé of human trafficking, forced labor, and sexual exploitation.

John Bowe, *Nobodies: Modern American Slave Labor and the Dark Side of the New Global Economy*. New York: Random House, 2007. Survey of slavery-like practices in the US.

David Brion Davis, *Inhuman Bondage: The Rise and Fall of Slavery in the New World*. Oxford: Oxford University Press, 2006. The Yale scholar's magisterial summary of decades of research on slavery.

Henry Louis Gates, Jr, ed., *The Classic Slave Narratives*. New York: Signet, 2002. Collection of firsthand testimonies of the slave experience.

Adam Hochschild, *Bury the Chains: Prophets and Rebels in the Fight to Free an Empire's Slaves*. Boston, MA: Houghton Mifflin, 2005. Fascinating account of the abolition movement and its contemporary resonance.

Chapter 5 – Arbitrary imprisonment

Anne Applebaum, *Gulag*. London: Penguin, 2003. Pulitzer Prize-winning account of the Soviet camp system.

Christian Solidarity Worldwide, 'North Korea: A Case to Answer, A Call to Act', Report, 2007. Report sampled in this chapter; available on the web at www.csw.org.uk/Countries/NorthKorea/Resources/North_Korea-A_Case_to_Answer-A_Call_to_Act.pdf

Tara Herivel and Paul Wright, eds, *Prison Nation: The Warehousing of America's Poor*. New York: Routledge, 2003. 'Makes a compelling case that the United States . . . operates its own gulag within this supposedly free society' (Edward S. Herman).

Jonathan Power, *Like Water on Stone: The Story of Amnesty International*. London: Penguin, 2001. Engaging and insightful history of Amnesty's evolution and operations.

Alexander Solzhenitsyn, *One Day in the Life of Ivan Denisovich*. London: Victor Gollancz, 1963. Solzhenitsyn, the Nobel Prizewinner, spent years in the Gulag; his lightly fictionalized account became a *cause célèbre* when published in Russia during the brief 'thaw' following Stalin's death. See also his three-volume masterwork, *The Gulag Archipelago*.

Chapter 6 – Torture

Amnesty International, *Torture in the Eighties*. London: Amnesty International, 1984. Trailblazing Amnesty report, issued at the height of torture's resurgence.

John Conroy, *Unspeakable Acts, Ordinary People: The Dynamics of Torture*. Berkeley, CA: University of California Press, 2001. Vivid exploration of torture in Great Britain, the US, and Israel.

Edward Peters, *Torture* (expanded edition). Philadelphia, PA: University of Pennsylvania Press, 1996. A very useful historical overview, now revised.

Elaine Scarry, *The Body in Pain: The Making and Unmaking of the World*. New York: Oxford University Press, 1985. Classic philosophical treatise.

Jacobo Timerman, *Prisoner without a Name, Cell without a Number*. New York: Alfred A. Knopf, 1981. Memoir of an Argentine newspaper editor who survived torture centers under military rule.

Philip Zimbardo, *The Lucifer Effect: Understanding How Good People Turn Evil*. New York: Random House, 2007. How 'ordinary' people can be conditioned to commit torture and abuse, by the creator of the famous Stanford Prison Experiment.

Chapter 7 – Rape and sexual crimes

Anonymous (trans. Philip Boehm), *A Woman in Berlin: Eight Weeks in the Conquered City*. New York: Metropolitan Books, 2005. Intensely personal account of the terrifying period following the Soviet conquest of Berlin, when rape of German women was the norm.

Susan Brownmiller, *Against Our Will: Men, Women, and Rape*. New York: Bantam, 1975. Groundbreaking discussion of rape.

R. Charli Carpenter, ed., *Born of War: Protecting Children of Sexual Violence Survivors in Conflict Zones*. Bloomfield, CT: Kumarian Press, 2007. The first volume on this important theme.

Human Rights Watch, *Shattered Lives: Sexual Violence during the Rwandan Genocide and its Aftermath*. New York: Human Rights Watch, September 1996. Early, detailed treatment of the sexual atrocities in Rwanda, available online at www.hrw.org/reports/1996/Rwanda.htm

Alexandra Stiglmayer, ed., *Mass Rape: The War Against Women in Bosnia-Herzegovina*. Lincoln, NE: University of Nebraska Press, 1994. Major edited collection on the crimes in Bosnia-Herzegovina.

Chapter 8 – Forced disappearance

Stephen Grey, *Ghost Plane: The True Story of the CIA Rendition and Torture Program*. New York: St. Martin's, 2007. The international network of 'black sites' for victims of US 'extraordinary rendition'.

Thomas Hauser, *Missing: The Execution of Charles Horman*. New York: Simon & Schuster, 1988. The disappearance of an American in Chile after the 1973 military coup; basis for the classic Costa-Gavras film.

John T. Parry, 'The Shape of Modern Torture: Extraordinary Rendition and Ghost Detainees', *Melbourne Journal of International Law*, 6 (2005), pp. 516–33. A cogent legal perspective.

John Simpson and Jana Bennett, *The Disappeared: Voices from a Secret War*. London: Robson Books, 1985. Journalistic account of crimes against humanity under the Argentine military regime of 1976–83.

Chapter 9 – Apartheid

Jimmy Carter, *Palestine: Peace Not Apartheid*. New York: Simon & Schuster, 2007. Controversial analysis of the Israeli–Palestinian conflict by the ex-US president.

Nancy L. Clark and William H. Worger, *South Africa: The Rise and Fall of Apartheid*. London: Longman, 2004. Probably the best textbook-style treatment.

Nelson Mandela, *Long Walk to Freedom: The Autobiography of Nelson Mandela*. Boston, MA: Back Bay Books, 1995. The life of the leader of anti-apartheid forces, who spent twenty-seven years in jail and emerged to serve as the first president of a democratic South Africa.

Allister Sparks, *The Mind of South Africa*. New York: Ballantine Books, 1990. Highly readable historical overview, with a focus on the post-1948 era.

Index

Abolition of Slavery Act (1833)
    60, 134
Abolitionist movement 61–62
Abrams, Jason 138
Abu Ghraib (prison) 100, 154
Afghanistan 130, 148–49
Africa Action 145–47
African National Congress
    (ANC) x, 86, 138, 142
African Rights 111
Afrikaners 132, 134–35
Aggressive war 15
Akayesu, Jean-Paul 10, 16, 19,
    73, 111
Al-Qa'eda 53
Albania 30
Alexander, Titus 145–46
Algeria 85, 95–97, 128
Algiers, battle of 96
Allen, Beverly 110
Allende, Salvador 126
American Civil Liberties Union
    (ACLU) 130
Améry, Jean 94
Amin, Idi 29, 95
Amnesty International ix, 18,
    86–89, 99, 126, 128,
    129–30, 152
Anderson, Benedict 115
Anfal campaign 52
Angola 141

ANZACS 1
Anti-Slavery Society 67, 152
Apartheid ix–x, 13, 16,
    132–50, 152, 157
    see also Gender apartheid,
    Global apartheid
Apartheid Convention (UN)
    (1973) 138–39, 150
Arar, Maher 130
Arbitrary imprisonment,
    see Imprisonment
Argentina 88, 94, 124–26, 128
Armenians 1–2, 16, 24, 27, 41
Artists United Against
    Apartheid 142
Aryan/Aryans 117, 133
Assyrians 1, 24
Atlantic slavery 57, 59
Auschwitz-Birkenau (death
    camp) 25, 83
Auschwitz III-Monowitz (labor
    camp) 58, 76–77
Australia 1, 28, 31, 132

Balkans 29, 41–42, 68, 72,
    108, 112, 119, 156
Balkars 45
Baltic states 45
Bangladesh 29, 107, 116
Bantustans 132

Barbarity, as legal term 27
Bardach, Janusz 80
Bass, Gary Jonathan 15
Bassiouni, M. Cherif 17
Belgium 64
Belgrade 49
Belo, Carlos Felipe Ximenes
    30–31
Benenson, Peter 86
Bengalis 107
Bible 20
"Black sites" 129–30
Blades, Ruben 126
Boers/Boer War 134
Bonnet, François 81
Bono 142
Booker, Salih 145–46
Boot, Machteld 37
Bosnia-Herzegovina (Bosnia
    and Herzegovina)/
    Bosnians xii, 12, 30, 35,
    36, 47–51, 108–09, 112,
    116, 129
Bophuthatswana 136, 137,
    142
Boudella, Hadj 129
Brazil 62, 70, 124
"Bringing Them Home"
    (report) 28
Broederbond (South Africa) 135
Brookes (slave ship) 6, 59, 62
Brownmiller, Susan 107
Bulgarian uprising 42
Burke, Edmund 104
Bush, George W. 99, 101–03,
    130, 154
Bybee, Jay 101
Bystanders 102–03, 122

Cameroon 69, 85
Cambodia 29, 74, 96
Canada 75, 117, 130
Cape Colony 134
Carpenter, R. Charli 116
Carter, Jimmy 143–44
Castro, Fidel 145
Catalyzing ideas x, 156
Catholicism 91, 125
Caucasus/Caucasians 45, 48
Central Intelligence Agency
    (CIA) 100–02, 129–30
Chandler, David 156
Chattel slavery 57, 60, 66, 67,
    68
Chechnya/Chechens 45–46
Cheney, Dick 100
Chetniks (paramilitaries)
    108–09
Children's rights 116
Chile 124, 126, 154
China/Chinese 8, 12, 32–33,
    37, 65–66, 70, 72, 74, 81,
    106, 107, 117, 149
Christian Solidarity Worldwide
    37, 82–84
Civil rights 104, 122
Civil War (US) 62–63, 133
Clarkson, Thomas 62
Clinton, Bill 31
Cold War 29, 31, 123, 141, 142
Colombia 124, 128, 131
Colonialism 2, 5, 20–23,
    28–29, 37, 41, 46, 63,
    75, 85, 92, 95–97, 122,
    132, 134, 138, 139, 144,
    146
"Comfort women" 107

Communism/communist 24, 30, 45, 74, 78, 81, 84, 87, 92, 121, 136, 141
See also China, North Korea, Soviet Union
Concentration camps 6
Constantinople, war-crimes trials in 2
Congo/Congolese xii, 6, 64, 84, 113–15
Congo Reform Association 64
Conrad, Joseph 64
"Constructive engagement" 141
Convention against Torture and Other Cruel, Inhuman or Degrading Treatment or Punishment, *see* Torture Convention
Convention on Forced Disappearance of Persons (OAS) (1994) 128
Convention on the Prevention and Punishment of the Crime of Genocide (UN) (1948), *see* Genocide Convention
Convention on Slavery, Servitude, Forced Labor, and Similar Institutions (1926) 64–65
Convention on the Suppression and Punishment of the Crime of Apartheid (UN) (1973), *see* Apartheid Convention
Corvée, *see* Forced labor
Cosmopolitanism x, 4, 6–7, 146, 156–57

Costa-Gavras 126
Cultural genocide 27
Crimes against peace 9, 15
Croatia/Croats 30, 48, 55, 108–09
Cuba 62, 141
Cuito Cuanavale, battle of 141

Dachau (concentration camp) 75
Dallaire, Roméo 26
Danner, Mark 47
Darfur 6, 14, 32–33, 113
Dautricourt, Joseph 19, 156
Dayton peace accords 48–49
de Klerk, F.W. 142
de Vabres, Henri Donnedieu 156
Death camps 75–77
Death penalty 12
Death squads 53, 101, 124–25, 128, 131, 154
Debt peonage 63–64
Declaration on the Protection of All Persons from Enforced Disappearance (UN) (1992) 126–27
Decolonization 5, 63, 138, 139
Democracy/democratic 74–75, 80, 84–86, 88, 95–97, 99–102, 104, 126, 144, 154
Democratic Party (US) 130
Deportation, *see* Forced deportation
Dergue 37
Destalinization 80
Dili massacre 30

Disease, as genocidal mechanism 21–22
Dizdarevic, Nadja 129
Dominican Republic 21, 87
Dostoevsky, Fyodor 77
Doyle, Sir Arthur Conan 64
Drakulic, Slavenka 108–09
Dube, Lucky 141
Dutch 21, 132, 134, 151
Dutch Reformed Church 134–35

East Pakistan, *see* Bangladesh
East Timor 30–32, 37–38, 152
East Timor Action Network (ETAN) 32
El Salvador 123
"Elements of Crimes", *see* Rome Statute
Elkins, Caroline 85
Endabuse.org 69
"Enhanced interrogation" 103
Enlightenment 91, 97
Enslavement, *see* Slavery
Equatorial Guinea 84
Equiano, Olaudah 61, 152
Ethiopia 37
"Ethnic cleansing" 6, 30, 43–56, 105–06, 108, 113, 115, 119
Eugenics 117, 133
European Court of Human Rights (ECHR) 99
European Union (EU) 49, 99
Extermination xii, 3, 9, 13, 15, 34–39, 40, 74, 75, 76, 79, 83, 110, 119, 132, 155

"Extraordinary rendition" 85, 102, 129–30

Falanga 91
Famine 37, 81
Farrow, Mia 33
Fascism/fascist 84, 92, 121
see also Nazis
Female infanticide/feticide 149
Feminism 107, 110, 112, 119, 148
Feminist Majority Foundation 148
Finns 45
Five Year Plans (Soviet Union) 65
Forced deportation/expulsion 13, 15, 43–44, 46
Forced disappearance 13, 85, 88, 121–31, 154
Forced exile 123
Forced labor viii, 20, 36, 58, 63, 65, 68, 70, 74, 76–84, 140
Forced Labor Convention 65
Forced population transfer/expulsion, *see* "Ethnic cleansing"
Forced pregnancy 13, 105, 108, 115–16
Forced sterilization 116–17
Foucault, Michel 90
France/French 1, 10, 21, 42, 60–61, 85, 90, 91, 95–97
Free the Slaves 67
French Revolution 10, 60
Fujimori, Alberto 154

Gandhi, Indira 117
Gas chambers 75
Gender apartheid 148–50
General Assembly (UN) 14, 126–27
Geneva Conventions (1949) 10, 18, 97
Genocidal intent 36, 155
Genocidal rape 110
Genocidal slavery 58–59
Genocide ix, xii, 6, 19–36, 38, 40, 43–44, 47, 58, 74, 75–77, 79, 83, 85, 106, 113, 118–19, 138, 151, 152, 155–56
 see also Genocide Convention
Genocide Convention (1948) xii, 10, 15, 16, 17–18, 19, 20, 28, 34–36, 38, 43–44, 84, 154
Germany/Germans 17, 24, 41, 45–47, 65, 75, 103, 106, 121–22, 130, 133
 see also Nazis
German South West Africa, *see* Namibia
Gestapo 93, 103, 121
Gladstone, William 42
Glasnost 141
Global apartheid 145–47, 150
Global North 5, 70, 146
Global South 5, 146, 150
Globalization 4, 6, 66, 70, 153, 157
Goldhagen, Daniel 76
Gorbachev, Mikhail 141
Great Britain/British 4, 30, 41, 52, 60–61, 71, 85, 88, 104, 117, 132, 133–34, 139, 154
Great Depression 151
Great Leap Forward (China) 65
Great Trek (South Africa) 134
Greater Asian Co-Prosperity Sphere 65
"Greatest generation" 151
Greek war of independence 41–42
Greeks 1, 24, 42, 45, 54–55
Group Areas Act (South Africa) (1950) 135
Guantánamo Bay 129
Guatemala 87, 123, 128
Gulag (Soviet Union) 65, 77–81, 123
 see also North Korea
Gulf War (1991) 52
Gypsies, *see* Roma

Habeas corpus 122
Habibie, B.J. 31
Habyarimana, Juvénal 111
Hague Conventions (1899, 1907) 7
Haiti/Haitian revolution 21, 60
Halliday, Denis 38
Handicapped 117
Harrison, David 71
Helsinki Final Agreement (1975) 97
Helsinki Watch 88
Hersh, Seymour 100

Himmler, Heinrich 121
Hispaniola, *see* Haiti,
  Dominican Republic
Hitler, Adolf 24, 75
Hochschild, Adam 62
Holmes, John 113–14
Holocaust, *see* Jews/Jewish
  Holocaust
Holy Inquisition 91
Homelands (South Africa) 132,
  136, 137, 142, 144, 145,
  149
  See also Bophuthatswana,
  Transkei
Homosexuals 8, 24, 117
Horman, Charles 126
Howard, Young 82
Hugo, Victor 92
Human rights xii, xiii, 2–3,
  5–6, 7–8, 17, 20, 26, 29,
  81, 84, 86, 88, 97, 98, 99,
  122, 124, 127, 129, 131,
  140, 145, 151, 153, 155
  see also Rights of man,
  Universal Declaration of
  Human Rights, Women's
  rights
Human Rights Watch 86, 88,
  130
Human trafficking/smuggling
  viii, 57, 67–73, 106, 112
Humanitarian intervention 29,
  31, 156
  see also Peacekeepers/
  peacekeeping
Hunt, Lynn xi
Hussein, Saddam 52–54, 101,
  128, 154

Hutus, *see* Rwanda

I.G. Farben 76
Iglesias, Julio 142
Illegal drugs 63
"Imagined communities" 115
Imprisonment 65, 74–89, 92,
  97, 118, 140
Indentured labor viii
India/Indians 37, 52, 117–18,
  135, 142, 149
Indigenous/aboriginal peoples
  4, 20–23, 28–29, 41, 54,
  59, 117, 132
Indirect killing 36–37
Indonesia 30–31, 37
  see also East Timor
Ingush 45
Inter-American Court of
  Human Rights (IACHR)
  99
Interahamwe (militia) 111
International Committee of the
  Red Cross (ICRC) 18,
  86
International Convention on
  the Suppression and
  Punishment of the Crime
  of Apartheid, *see*
  Apartheid Convention
International Convention on
  the Prevention and
  Punishment of the Crime
  of Genocide, *see* Genocide
  Convention
International Court of Justice
  (ICJ) 12

International Criminal Court (ICC) xiii, 11–14, 34, 68, 105, 154, 155

International Criminal Tribunal for the Former Yugoslavia (ICTY) 11, 29, 35, 36, 109–10, 155

International Criminal Tribunal for Rwanda (ICTR) 10–11, 19, 111, 155

International governmental organizations (IGOs) x–xi, 33

International Law Commission (UN) 35

International regimes 5, 29, 103–04

see also Prohibition regimes

Iran 149

Iraq/Iraqis 24, 33, 38, 52–53, 97, 100–01, 128–29, 154, 156

Irish Republican Army (IRA) 104

Irredentism 54

Israel/Israelis 13, 17, 54, 85, 143–45, 150

Jackson, Robert 15

Janjaweed (militia) 33

Japan/Japanese 8, 11, 65, 68, 81, 96, 106, 107, 121

Jerusalem 144

Jews/Jewish Holocaust 8, 15, 24–25, 46, 65, 75–77, 83, 110, 117, 121, 133, 143–45

see also Israel/Israelis

"Jim Crow" 63, 133

Kafka, Franz 92

Kang, Cheol-Hwan 82

Kant, Immanuel 4

Karachays 45

Keitel, Wilhelm 121

Kemal, Mestafa (Ataturk) 42

Kenya 84–85

Khmer Rouge, *see* Cambodia

Kim Il Sung 81

Kim Jong Il 81

Kissinger, Henry 154

Klein, Naomi 101

Kohler, Gernot 145

Kolyma (labor camps) 78–80

Korea/Koreans 107

See also North Korea

Kosovo/Kosovars 30–31, 41, 47

Krajina 48

Krstic, Radislav 35

Kuper, Leo 79

Kurds 52–53, 54

Ladysmith Black Mambazo 141–42

Lamyks 45

Land Act (South Africa) (1913) 134, 138, 144

Laos 96

Las Madres, see Mothers of the Plaza de Mayo

Law for the Prevention of Offspring with Hereditary

Diseases (Germany) (1933) 117
League of Nations 4, 12, 64
Lelyveld, Joseph 145
Lemkin, Raphael ix, 26–28, 152
Lemmon, Jack 126
Lenin, Vladimir 77–78
Leopold, King (Belgium) 64
Levi, Primo 76–77
Liberalism 97
Liberia 14
Lieberman, Benjamin 54
Locke, John 91
Luban, David 3

Macedonia 30
MacKinnon, Catharine 110
MacMillan, Harold 139
Magna Carta 5
Makeba, Miriam 142
Mandela, Nelson x, 86, 137, 142
Mandelstam, Nadezhda 123
Mann, Michael 43
Mao Zedong/Maoism 37, 65, 82
Maquiladoras 66
Marcus, David 37
Marley, Bob xii
Martens Clause, *see* Hague Conventions
Masekela, Hugh 142
Masri, Khaled 130
Mau-Mau uprising 85
Mauritania 67
Mauthausen (labor camp) 58
Mbeki, Thabo 145

Mead, Margaret x
Medic, Richard 55
Memorial (organization) 78
Mens rea 11
Mesopotamia, *see* Iraq
Mexico 70
Military conscription 44, 65
Mill, John Stuart x
Milosevic, Slobodan 14
Minter, William 145–46
Morel, E.D. xii
Mostar 55–56
Mothers of the Disappeared, *see* Mothers of the Plaza de Mayo
Mothers of the Plaza de Mayo x, 99, 125–26
Mozambique 85
Mukwege, Denis 114
Multinational corporations 5, 38

Nacht und Nebel, *see* "Night and Fog"
Nadelmann, Ethan 62
Naimark, Norman 40
Namibia 58, 132, 141
National Endowment for Democracy 83
National Liberation Front (FLN) 96
National Party (South Africa) 133, 141
National Security State 123
National Socialism, *see* Nazis
NATO (North Atlantic Treaty Organization) 30–31

Nazis/nazism 6, 8, 11, 15, 16–17, 24–25, 26, 27, 29, 44–46, 65, 74, 75–77, 92–94, 96, 103, 110, 117, 121, 134
Neanderthals 20
Nepal 128
New Zealand 1, 132
Nicholas II (czar) 77
Nigeria 71
"Night and Fog" 121–22, 129
Nobel Peace Prize 31, 88
Nongovernmental organizations (NGOs) ix, 5, 33, 86, 99, 145, 148, 153
Norilsk (labor camps) 79
Norm entrepreneurs 5, 27, 39, 56, 62, 88, 153
Norm grafting 62, 89, 145, 150, 155
North Korea 37, 74, 81–84
Novels, role of xi
Nuremberg tribunal xii, 8–10, 14–16, 19, 34, 106, 122, 153–54, 156

Obote, Milton 29
Oketch, Richard Juma 95
Olympic Games 32–33
Organization of American States (OAS) 99, 128
Organization for Security and Cooperation in Europe (OSCE) 55
"Other inhumane acts" 13, 17–18, 155, 157

Ottoman Empire 1–2, 7, 16, 24, 27, 41–42, 52, 58, 153
see also Turkey/Turks

Pakistan 149, 151
Palestine/Palestinians 52, 54, 85, 143–45
Patterson, Orlando 59
Peacekeepers/peacekeeping 6, 26, 30, 33, 48, 114
Pearl Harbor 121
Pearl River Delta (China) 66
Peña Valdez, Julio de 87
Perestroika 141
Persecution 13, 15, 17–18, 155
Peru 154
Philippines/Filipinos 72, 107
Pieds noirs 96
Pinochet, Augusto 14, 126, 154
Planespotters 130
Poland 17, 27, 46, 75, 121
Pontecorvo, Gillo 97
Portugal/Portuguese 21, 30, 86, 139
Potocari 49, 51
Pregnancy, *see* Forced pregnancy
Priest, Dana 130
Principled-issue networks ix, 152
Prisoners of war 10, 25, 46, 79
Prohibition regimes viii, ix, 5–6, 12, 62, 72, 86, 103–04, 130, 153, 156
Protestantism 91

Queen 142

Ramos-Horta, José 31
Rape, *see* Sexual
    crimes/exploitation
Rape of Nanjing 106
Ratner, Steven 138
Reconciliation 54–56
Reconstruction (US) 63, 133
Red Berets (paramilitaries) 50
Red Cross, *see* International
    Committee of the Red
    Cross
Redhouse, Diana 86
Reeves, Eric 32
Republika Srpska 49
Residential schools 28
Responsibility to protect 3
Rhodesia 141
Rights of Man xi
Rivonia trials 137–38
Robinson, Darryl 13, 34
Roma 8, 46, 117
Rome Statute (ICC) (1998)
    xiii, 11–14, 16, 18, 34, 37,
    40, 57, 67, 68, 72–73, 105,
    112, 115, 116–17, 155
    see also International
    Criminal Court
Rousseau, Jean-Jacques xi
Rule of law 80, 91, 102, 123,
    127
Rumsfeld, Donald 154
Russia 30, 46, 77, 81, 85, 128
    see also Soviet Union
Rwanda 25–26, 110–12, 113,
    118

Rwanda tribunal, *see*
    International Criminal
    Tribunal for Rwanda
    (ICTR)
Rwandan Patriotic Front
    (RPF) 25, 111

Sainte-Marie, Buffy 22–23
Sanctions 38, 141, 152
Sarajevo 49, 55, 129
Saudi Arabia 149
Sazonov, Sergei 1
Schwesig, Karl 93
Security Council (UN) 38,
    109
Segregation 5, 135, 138, 139,
    144, 148–49,
Self-determination 5
Separate Amenities Act (South
    Africa) (1953) 135
Serbia/Serbs 12, 30, 41,
    47–51, 55, 108–09
Sexual enslavement 73, 105,
    111–13, 155
Sexual crimes/exploitation ix,
    13, 44, 57, 72–73, 74,
    105–20, 133, 155
    see also Sexual enslavement
Sharpeville massacre 138
Shaw, Martin 19, 44
Shi'a Muslims 52–33, 101, 128
Sierra Leone 14
Sikkink, Katherine 124
Silk Road 58
Silverman, Lisa 91
Sivakumaran, Sandesh 119
Simon, Paul 142

Six-Day War 143
Slave labor, *see* Slavery
Slavery viii, ix, 9, 13, 15, 25,
    36, 57–73, 75–76, 79, 82,
    133–34, 152, 153, 155,
    157
    See also Sexual enslavement
"Slavery-like practices" 57, 68
Slavs 8, 24–25, 46, 117
Smyrna (Izmir) 42
Socialism/socialist 29, 121,
    123, 126,
South Africa ix, x, 85, 87,
    132–50, 152, 157
Soviet Koreans 45
Soviet Union 8, 17, 25, 27,
    37, 44–46, 48, 65, 74,
    77–81, 87, 92–93, 106,
    123, 141
    see also Russia
Soweto 141
Spacek, Sissy 126
Spain/Spanish 21, 63, 87, 154
Springsteen, Bruce 142
Srebrenica massacre 30–31, 35,
    48–49, 51, 109
Sri Lanka 128
Stalin, Joseph/Stalinism 45,
    47, 58, 65, 78, 82, 93,
    123
STAND (Students Taking
    Action Now–Darfur)
    32–33
State sovereignty 12, 13,
    15–16, 153
State terror 92, 104, 123
Stewart, Rod 142
Sting 126

Stowe, Harriet Beecher xi–xii
Structural violence/inequality
    38–39, 150
Sudan 32–33
    see also Darfur
Suharto 30
Sullivan, Andrew 103
Sun City 142
Sunni Muslims 52–53, 54,
    101, 128
Suppression of Communism
    Act (South Africa) (1950)
    136
Syria 24, 130

Talaat Pasha 27
Taliban 148–49
Tanzania 29
Tatars 45
Tehlirian, Soghomon 27
Terrorism/terrorist 41, 53, 54,
    100, 104, 133, 143
Thailand 72
"Third World" 96, 101, 118
Thurston, Robert 45
Tibet 117
Tokyo tribunal 8, 16, 106
Torture x, 6, 13, 16, 74, 88,
    90–104, 122, 124, 127,
    140, 154, 155
Torture Convention (UN)
    (1984) 98–99, 101
Totalitarianism 44, 75, 80, 81,
    92–93, 104, 133
Transkei 136
Treaty of Sèvres 42
Treblinka (death camp) 75

Truth and Reconciliation
     Commission for East
     Timor (UN) 37
Tu quoque 106
Turkey/Turks 42–43, 45,
     54–55
Turkmen 53, 54
Tutsis, *see* Rwanda
Tutu, Desmond 143

U2 126, 142
Uganda 29, 84–85, 95
Ukraine 45
United Kingdom (UK), *see*
     Great Britain
United Nations (UN) ix, x, 4,
     12, 26, 31, 37–38, 48, 57,
     114, 126–27, 152
United States (US) 4, 12, 26,
     29, 30, 41, 52, 59, 61,
     62–63, 65–66, 69, 70, 75,
     81, 85–86, 87, 88, 97,
     99–104, 117, 121, 123,
     128–30, 133, 135, 141
Universal Declaration of
     Human Rights (UN)
     (1948) 10, 15, 97, 127,
     154
Urbina, Ian 143
Urkas 80
Uruguay 124
Umkhonto we Sizwe 138

Van Zandt, Steven 142
Vandalism, as legal term 27
Vasiljevic, Mitar 36

Versailles treaty (1919) 24
Vidal-Naquet, Pierre 104
Vietnam 29, 96
Villaflor, Azucena 125
Voltaire 91, 151
Vorkuta (labor camps) 79

Wage slavery 66
Waldron, Jeremy 101
War crimes 8–9, 12, 155
"War on terror" 6, 85, 97, 99,
     104, 128–31, 157
Waterboarding 100–01
West Bank 143–44, 150
West Pakistan 107
White Eagles (paramilitaries) 50
"White slavery" 72
Wiesel, Elie 76
Wines, Michael 84
Witchcraft 91
Women/women's rights x,
     107–08, 113, 148–50
     see also Human trafficking/
     smuggling, Sexual
     crimes/exploitation
World Conference Against
     Racism 143
World War I 1, 10, 12, 24, 27,
     41, 42, 77, 153
World War II 8, 12, 16, 24,
     26, 29, 44–47, 65, 75, 81,
     97, 101, 106, 114, 117,
     124, 134, 138
Wright, Ronald 20

Yoo, John 103

Yugoslav tribunal, *see*
    International Criminal
    Tribunal for the Former
    Yugoslavia
Yugoslavia 12, 29, 47, 49, 52,
    56, 108, 128
    see also Bosnia-Herzegovina/

Bosnians, Croatia/Croats,
    Kosovo/Kosovars,
    Macedonia, Serbia/Serbs

Zambia 84
Zimbabwe 141